THE LIGHTING PRIMER

THE LIGHTING PRIMER

BERNARD R. BOYLAN, P.E.

IOWA STATE UNIVERSITY PRESS AMES, IOWA

DEDICATED TO **BECKY and NICKY,** the lights of our lives

After graduation from the United States Naval Academy in 1950 with a B.S. in Engineering, **Bernard R. Boylan** served in the Navy during the Korean conflict and then joined the General Electric Company. Since then he has conducted lectures, workshops, and educational programs on all aspects of lighting. He has taught lighting courses to engineers, contractors, and salespeople at the Chicago Lighting Institute and to interior designers at the College of DuPage and is currently conducting a course in the Department of Architecture at the University of Notre Dame. He is a Registered Professional Engineer in the State of Illinois and has received the Distinguished Service Award from the Illuminating Engineering Society of North America.

© 1987 Iowa State University Press, Ames, Iowa 50010
All rights reserved

Composed by Iowa State University Press
Printed in the United States of America

No part of this book may be reproduced in any form or by any electronic or mechanical means, including information storage and retrieval systems, without written permission from the publisher, except for brief passages quoted in a review.

First edition, 1987
Second printing, 1988

Library of Congress Cataloging-in-Publication Data

Boylan, Bernard R., 1927–
   The lighting primer.

   Bibliography: p.
   Includes index.
   1. Lighting, Architectural and decorative. I. Title.
TH7703.B76   1987   747'.92   87-2664
ISBN 0-8138-1092-2

CONTENTS

PREFACE, vii

1. FUNDAMENTALS, 3

2. GENERAL TERMS, 7

3. COLOR, 10

4. LAMPS, 15

5. CONTROL OF LIGHT, 42

6. FIXTURES, 46

7. LIGHTING CONTROLS, 54

8. COSTS, 57

9. CALCULATIONS, 61

10. QUANTITY AND QUALITY, 86

11. GENERAL APPLICATIONS, 92

12. RESIDENCES, 95

13. OFFICES, 108

14. STORES AND OTHER APPLICATIONS, 117

vi

APPENDIX: LAMP CATALOG, 126

GLOSSARY, 137

REFERENCES AND FURTHER READING, 144

INDEX, 145

PREFACE

THE NEED FOR THIS BOOK became apparent to the author when he was asked to teach a course in illumination to an interior design class. Previous instructors had managed with manufacturer's literature or had done without any reference material at all. Most books presently used as texts are fine for reference but unacceptable for classroom use because of confusing, unrequired data; use of illuminating engineering terms to the exclusion of language in everyday use; or incomplete explanations.

Engineering writings on illumination have evolved over the years from deliberations of the various technical committees of the Illuminating Engineering Society of North America. The resultant design methods accent needlessly accurate calculations, even with estimated input, and generally neglect the human aspects of lighting. Application techniques and hardware descriptions lag current practice by several years because of the necessarily slow flow of information from the committees.

Books written by designers and architects tend to contain many of the same little-used engineering tables, diagrams, and formulas found in the more technical works. In addition, they are often rife with photos and sketches that contribute little basic understanding to the novice in the field of lighting. The systems illustrated are often limited to tracklights and downlights, even when used for unsuitable work situations.

Although the everyday language used here instead of trade jargon may offend purists in both the design and engineering fields, this book attempts to offer a compromise between the two approaches described above. Calculations, although still painful to many nonengineers, are explained and simplified to be no more accurate than needed for a reasonable forecast of light levels and resultant brightnesses. Human, design, and architectural aspects are presented, and a useful knowledge of light and its manipulation is imparted in everyday language.

Light bulbs, fixtures, ballasts, and controls for the light itself and the lighting system (that is, the hardware of a lighting system) are important to successful design and treated in some depth. Common misconceptions regarding beneficial and detrimental effects of light sources are demystified.

The costs of light, initial and operating, are often misunderstood and viewed from only one aspect, while fixture price, lamp life, and most important, electric rates, among other variables, can have important effects on overall economics. While these costs have been historically left to the judgment of engineers, other members of the design team should be cognizant of their effects before a plan is finalized. Basic costing methods are presented along with convenient estimating tools.

What light is, what it is not, and how it acts are clarified by experience resulting from 30 years of daily contact with the electrical industry, the design community, and the general public. Vision and its importance in gathering information from our environment is explained along with the way quality as well as quantity of light affects the speed and accuracy of our seeing.

Use of light in homes, offices, and stores to help perform the seeing tasks encountered in these spaces and to assist design and human considerations is outlined here, but sources for more detailed explanations are given in the list of References and Further Reading at the end of the book.

THE
LIGHTING
PRIMER

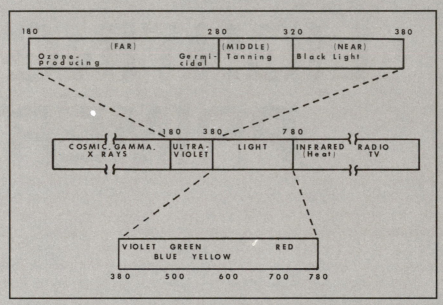

1.1. This chart shows how light relates to the rest of the electro-magnetic spectrum. Nanometers or angstroms (there are 10 angstroms per nanometer) are used as measurements for wavelengths near those of light, although frequency (in hertz or cycles per second) defines other portions of the spectrum.

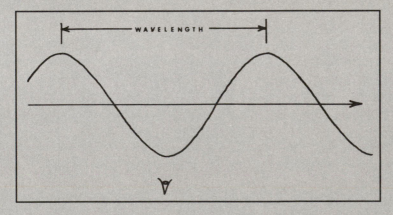

1.2. Wavelength is the distance from peak to peak (or valley to valley) of the energy wave, while frequency is the number of waves passing a point (indicated by the eye) in a period of time, normally the second.

1

FUNDAMENTALS

THIS DISCUSSION OF THE NATURE of radiant energy—including light, how it acts, and how we react to that energy—will provide a sound basis for succeeding chapters.

THE SPECTRUM

Figure 1.1 shows divisions of the electromagnetic spectrum, of which light is a part. The numbers on the chart are distances, in nanometers, from peak to peak of energy waves, which can be imagined to be just like waves in the ocean (Figure 1.2). Both types of waves carry power from one place to another and both have peaks and valleys. The distance from one wave top to the next is called its wavelength, while the number of peaks passing a given point in a second is known as frequency, in cycles per second or hertz. Frequency in units of megahertz, kilohertz, and hertz is used to designate radio, television, and electrical power, while wavelength in nanometers is used for light and nearby portions of the spectrum.

The portions of the spectrum labeled light, infrared, and ultraviolet are situated near the center of the band and generated by some type of electric lamp (see Figure 4.22) as well as by other sources. While there are variations, the divisions shown in Figure 1.1 indicate the generally accepted limits of each type of energy.

Ultraviolet radiation is divided into three portions that are, with no imagination whatsoever, named near, middle, and far. Near ultraviolet, or black light, is situated right next to violet-colored light. Black light is the energy that produces somewhat weird effects in head shops, bars, and other such locations. A source filtered to absorb visible light produces only a dull blue light, but the near ultraviolet emitted causes certain materials to take on brilliant colors. Starch used for stiffening fabrics, for example, emits a brilliant blue color when exposed to black light. Some materials used in false teeth turn chartreuse under black light.

Middle, or erythemal, ultraviolet is the stuff that tans and burns skin. Ordinary glass, used for most lamps, filters out this portion of the spectrum, but there are some mercury and fluorescent sources, called sunlamps, that are designed to generate tanning rays and should be used with extreme caution because of the possibility of sunburn.

Far ultraviolet radiation is truly dangerous to humans. Included is the germicidal range, which as the name implies, kills germs. It also causes "eyeball sunburn," which is temporarily painful but not permanently damaging. This portion of the spectrum is widely used in drug production to eliminate random bacteria and in communicable disease wards of hospitals to protect staff and visitors in those dangerous areas. Lamps made primarily for ozone production were once widely used in clothes driers and air purifiers to get that fresh-air, after-the-thunderstorm smell; but these passed from the scene when it became recognized that ozone is a poisonous gas in sufficient concentration.

Light itself has been defined in several ways over the centuries, with two explanations surviving. One, the corpuscular theory, holds that light is composed of matter called photons and that energy is transferred from place to place by this material. This theory is used by physicists when the other one does not work. The other one, which we shall use, pictures light as part of the electromagnetic spectrum, which as explained earlier, transfers energy by wave motion.

The textbook definition of light is somewhat ponderous — visually evaluated radiant energy. Starting at the end of that phrase, light is "energy" because it heats objects it falls upon, "radiant" because it moves outward from its source in a straight line through all sorts of transparent media, and "visually evaluated" because it can be seen. The common term "ultraviolet light" is just plain wrong because ultraviolet energy produces no visual sensation.

Designations of light — called, of course, colors — have violet at the shortest wavelength and red at the longest. See Figure 1.1 for commonly accepted wavelength divisions and Figure 4.22 to choose the best source for a particular color.

Light is not visible until it reflects from something — dust, water droplets, walls, anything, as long as the object reflects light. This fact of physics was apparently not understood too well by the planners of an exhibit widely billed at the most recent New York World's Fair as featuring a "several million candlepower beam of light that could be seen from Boston." However, if there was a cloudless, dry night the beam could not be seen at all, much less forever, because there was nothing for the light to reflect from. The brightnesses we see and interpret as images are caused by light reflected from some more or less solid object.

EYES

The versatility and adaptability of those two instruments called eyes are truly marvelous. We receive information about our surroundings from the other senses, to be sure, but it is sight that gathers a very high percentage of our perceptions. While the comfortable temperature range for most people is somewhere between 60 and 80 degrees Fahrenheit, human sight can operate with reasonable efficiency in light levels all the way from half a footcandle (moonlight) to 5000 or more footcandles in full sunlight. Most clerical tasks could be performed very comfortably in the shade of a tree, with relatively even brightnesses in view from the grass, sky, and other surroundings and about 500 footcandles on the seeing task. This high a light level in interiors requires an extremely well-designed system for equal visual comfort. As a comparison between outdoor and indoor levels, much reading at home is done under less than 30 footcandles, while the same level outdoors occurs at dusk when we start turning on our headlights. Figure 1.3 shows our eye reaction to various colors of light, with highest sensitivity in the yellow-green area.

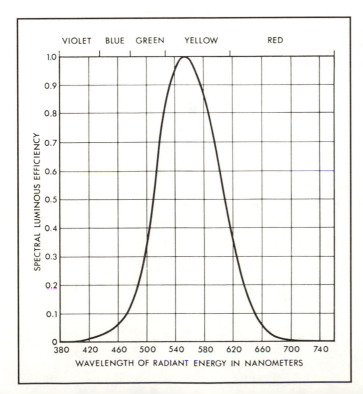

1.3.   Standard visibility curve of the human eye indicates sensitivity at various points in the visible spectrum. (*Courtesy of the Illuminating Engineering Society of North America*)

FACTORS OF SEEING

Certain conditions must be present for the sensation of sight to take place. Light, and something for it to bounce off are essential.

BRIGHTNESS. No matter how much light falls on a black object (one that reflects no light), there can be no visibility because there is no brightness. If there is no light the reflectance of objects does not matter. Brightness calculations are explained in Chapter 9.

CONTRAST. If everything in the field of view was exactly the same brightness, as might occur inside a giant Ping-Pong ball during a foggy snowstorm, visibility would literally stop at the end of one's arm. No matter how much brightness may be present, contrast (difference in brightness) is required for vision. White print on white paper simply disappears, for example.

SIZE. Another necessity for vision is size—not physical size, but angular size. Organisms too small to be seen with unaided vision become perfectly obvious under a microscope. The organisms have not become any larger, but their visual angle has been increased by the instrument. An elephant is quite apparent when it is ten feet away but disappears at a distance of several miles.

SPEED. The remaining factor is speed—visual, not actual. Because they move so fast, bullets coming out of a gun remain invisible even if the other three factors are present. There would be no point in lighting the area between the marksman and target in a shooting range because there is nothing to be seen out there. Old battleship sailors, however, can testify that 16-inch projectiles can be seen when fired from one's own ship but not from another vessel. The reason is that your own bullet is going directly away from you and appears almost motionless except for diminishing size, while the one from the other ship presents its full angular speed to you. Contrast and brightness have to be present for this example, of course. It would not work at night unless the shell was a tracer.

Although suitable brightness, contrast, size, and speed allow visibility, the eye sees a lot more than just what it is looking at, so accuracy and comfort of seeing require other factors. These are discussed in Chapter 10.

2

GENERAL TERMS

LEARNING SPECIALIZED TERMS is a chore, but such knowledge is essential for communication in any discipline. Fortunately, few such terms are in everyday use in lighting and are quite easily conquered.

Lamp, as used in the industry, does not mean that thing on your end table with the shade on it; it refers to a light bulb or tube. "Table," "floor," or "portable" are added to "lamp" to indicate the apparatus containing a light bulb.

Light output of a source is expressed in *lumens.* A 100-watt light bulb produces 1750 lumens; a 40-watt cool white fluorescent produces 3150. Lumens can be thought of as the measurement for the flow rate of light.

The efficiency (efficacy, in engineering terms) of light sources is measured by the amount of light emitted for each watt of power used, or *lumens per watt* (LPW). (Figure 4.21 and the lamp tables in the Appendix show LPW values for most sources.)

When one lumen of light falls on a 1-square-foot surface (an area equal to a square measuring 1 foot on each side), the resultant illumination level is one *footcandle.* All lighting calculations stem from that relationship: one footcandle equals one lumen per square foot. Expressed as a formula:

Footcandles = lumens per square foot

$$fc = lm/ft^2$$

Brightness (more correctly, luminance, in engineering parlance)—what you see when looking at something—is expressed in two ways, one used with low levels and one with high. The two different terms are in use only to make calculations easier to handle.

The terms *candle, candles per square inch, candela,* or *candlepower* (for high values), all used pretty much interchangeably, derive from the brightness of an ordinary candle and are used for high brightnesses like lamps, fixtures, and spotlights.

Footlambert (for low values) is the brightness term used for room surfaces and other relatively dull things. There are 452 footlamberts in a candle, or, stated another way, a candle is 452 times as bright as a footlambert. As explained below, a footlambert can be thought of as a reflected footcandle.

Reflectance, or *reflection factor* of a surface, in combination with the amount of light falling on that surface, determines its brightness. A perfectly black surface has a reflectance of zero and produces no brightness no matter how much light falls on it. A perfectly white surface, on the other hand, reflects all the light it intercepts and has a reflection factor of 1.00 or 100 percent. Since brightness equals light level in footcandles times the reflection factor, the white surface will have a brightness in footlamberts equal to its light level in footcandles. In formula form:

Footlamberts = footcandles × reflectance
fL = fc × rf

Some applications of these terms might be of interest. A good white paint, for example, has a reflectance of 85 percent. A white wall receiving 100 lumens per square foot would have a light level of 100 vertical footcandles (measurement can be made horizontally, vertically, or by any combination thereof), a reflectance of 85 percent, and therefore a brightness of 85 footlamberts:

100 fc × 0.85 = 85 fL

A tan typewriter with a reflection factor of 50 percent would have a brightness of 50 footlamberts in an office lighted to 100 footcandles:

100 fc × 0.50 = 50 fL

Approximate reflectances of common materials are shown in Table 2.1. Reflectances of some representative paint colors are given in the

TABLE 2.1.   Reflectances for some common surfaces

Material	Reflectance
Flat white paint	85%
Pastel colors	60
White ceiling tile	70
Aluminum paint	65
White porcelain enamel	85
Process aluminum	75
Stainless steel	60
Light wood	60
Concrete	20
Glass	15

Appendix. Paint manufacturers often indicate reflectances along with their color chips. Note that since glass is a poor reflector of light, window walls should be treated as having zero reflectance.

Reflectance can be measured as depicted in Figure 2.1 by placement of a light meter at the surface to be read with the cell first aimed away from the surface and then toward it. The ratio, or fraction, of footcandles bouncing off the surface to those impinging on it is the reflection factor:

$$rf = fc\ on/fc\ off$$

Distance of the meter from the wall is a critical factor during this procedure. If it is too close, shadows from the meter and the reader's body will cause low readings, as will too great a distance. Use the maximum reflected reading obtained when using this method.

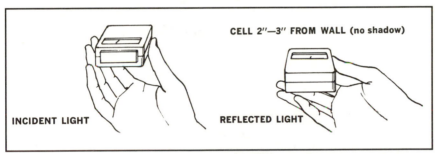

CELL 2″—3″ FROM WALL (no shadow)

INCIDENT LIGHT

REFLECTED LIGHT

2.1. A method of determining reflectance values of unknown room surfaces by use of a pocket light meter. The ratio of incident to reflected light equals reflectance of the surface. (*Courtesy of the General Electric Company*)

The terms defined above will be used throughout the rest of the book. Their application to lighting design and their relationship to each other are explained in Chapter 9.

3
COLOR

JUST AS THE ELECTROMAGNETIC SPECTRUM is divided into ultra-violet, infrared, light, and other forms of energy by wavelength or frequency, so light is subdivided by different wavelengths into colors. Light with the shortest wavelength, close to ultraviolet, we call violet. Then, in increasing wavelengths, come blue, green, yellow, orange, and ending at about 760 nanometers, red.

Mixing different light colors produces entirely different results than mixing pigments or dyes, as shown in Figure 3.1 (inside front cover). Light is changed by addition such that white light results from the proper mixture of red, green, and blue, while pigments produce black from the corresponding combination of magenta, cyan, and yellow. Note in Figure 3.1 that the primary colors of light are the secondary colors of pigments.

Color of light can be modified by either transmission or absorption, as discussed in Chapter 5. Red glass modifies light passing through it by absorbing all but the red rays, while red paint accomplishes the same thing by reflecting only the red ones. Yellow bug lights appear their characteristic color because paint on the bulb absorbs blue produced by the filament, passing only the wavelengths we see as yellow. (The reason they are called bug lights is that bugs see differently than people and are not attracted as much by yellow light as they are by blue.)

Reflectance of a surface is determined by its shade (amount of black) or by its tint (amount of white). Red or blue paint can be as good a reflector of light as yellow or green, providing the tint or shade is correct.

An important consideration in any discussion of color is our expectation of how things should appear. Sky should be blue; grass, lettuce, and spinach should be green; bananas, yellow. When they are not, we become disturbed. Who would consider drinking green beer except for one day a year? Lamp manufacturers have periodically introduced noticeably greenish, more efficient fluorescent lamps into the marketplace, but they have been emphatically rejected. While green foliage and room surfaces are cool, refreshing, and soothing, green light seems unnatural (and is unflattering). The dramatic arts take advantage of the effects of colored light by bathing villains in green while the good guys are lighted with red (or at least pink, which is flattering). Lights should be blue or yellow or pink, but not green.

COLOR TEMPERATURE

Apparent color temperature (or correlated color temperature) of a light source indicates its degree of blueness or redness as we view it, with the higher number of two being the bluer. This relationship is shown in Figure 3.2 (inside back cover). As noted in Figure

3.3. Apparent color temperatures of various common light sources in degrees Kelvin. On the Kelvin scale the higher the number, the bluer the source. See Figure 3.2 for a different representation.

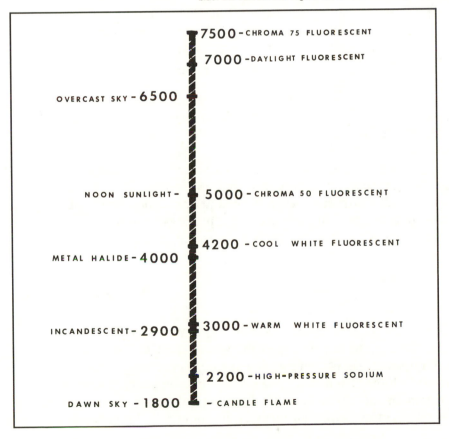

7500 - CHROMA 75 FLUORESCENT

7000 - DAYLIGHT FLUORESCENT

OVERCAST SKY - 6500

NOON SUNLIGHT - 5000 - CHROMA 50 FLUORESCENT

4200 - COOL WHITE FLUORESCENT

METAL HALIDE - 4000

INCANDESCENT - 2900 - 3000 - WARM WHITE FLUORESCENT

2200 - HIGH-PRESSURE SODIUM

DAWN SKY - 1800 - CANDLE FLAME

3.3, a candle flame has an apparent color temperature of about 1800 degrees Kelvin (a temperature scale that has its zero at -273 degrees Celsius and -434 degrees Fahrenheit), while incandescent lamps are about 2900, cool white fluorescent 4200, and an overcast sky approximately 6500 degrees Kelvin. Apparent color temperature gives no indication of a source's color-rendering ability or how pigments will appear when viewed under that source.

COLOR-RENDERING INDEX

Light sources other than incandescent are assigned a color-rendering index (CRI) number based on their ability to make pigments look as they would under certain test sources when compared to other sources having the same color temperature. Incandescent lamps are tacitly assigned a CRI at or near 100. The scale, while nowhere near perfect, is the only method we have that indicates how colors will look under a given source. Its use should be limited to lamps of the same color temperature, but it is common incorrect practice to compare sources with widely varying appearances. The index ranges from incandescent at the top, down through the good color fluorescents like cool white deluxe and 5000 degree Kelvin lamps, metal halide, cool white and warm white fluorescent, high-pressure sodium, and (at the very bottom because colors lighted by it cannot be distinguished) low-pressure sodium. See the lamp listing in the Appendix for the CRIs and apparent color temperatures of all common discharge lamps.

Energy output of sources is often represented in spectral power distribution (or spectral energy distribution) curves. While such curves are visually attractive when printed in color, they really indicate little about a lamp's appearance (color temperature) or its visual effect on pigments (CRI). Figure 3.4 shows such curves for two fluorescent colors.

"WHITE" LIGHT

Light sources called "white" abound in our society. There are greenish, bluish, pinkish, and goldish "white" light sources everywhere. Lamp catalogs list several dozen fluorescent lamps that are considered "white." Then there are several high-intensity discharge lamps—even including (with some imagination) high-pressure sodium—and the most "white" of them all, incandescent. Incandescent

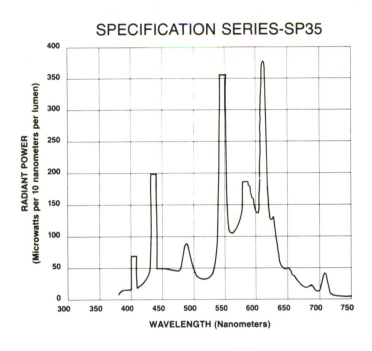

SPECIFICATION SERIES-SP35

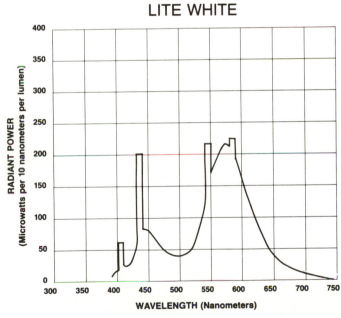

LITE WHITE

3.4. Spectral power distribution curves for two colors of fluorescent lamps. Sometimes called spectral energy distribution curves, they indicate the amount of energy emitted at each point in the electromagnetic spectrum. (*Courtesy of the General Electric Company*) lamps have even been considered "white" after their bulbs have been painted to absorb part of the spectrum. And, of course, ever-changing daylight is considered "white" even at its bluest or reddest. The official definition of "daylight," by the way, is that color of light extant at 12 o'clock noon on the twenty-first of June in the latitude of Washington, D.C., with 10 percent of the sky covered with clouds.

The roughly triangular diagram in Figure 3.2 was developed by CIE (International Commission on Illumination, an international organization devoted to color) to allow designation of colors on x-y coordinates. This is just one of several methods developed over the years to make color designation more scientific. The three basic colors blend near the center into "white" light, which can be produced by a whole range of sources.

Incandescent, certainly "white," emits a lot of red and very little blue light, while cool white fluorescent has an opposite output. The reason for such a wide range of acceptable sources is our ability to modify the colors we are viewing by the range of other colors we see at the same time. The eye becomes saturated by the majority of what it sees and distorts the rest. Most of us are familiar with the little experiment of looking at a picture for a while, looking away, and then seeing a reversed color image of the scene. Color saturation is roughly the same phenomenon. Almost any light source can be made to appear white, given the proper setting.

4
LAMPS

CHOICE OF THE PROPER LAMP for each application is probably the most important decision made by the designer of a lighting system. Color rendition, energy efficiency, cost, and general effectiveness of the installation are all affected by the attributes of the light source.

INCANDESCENT OR FILAMENT

One reason most of us feel that incandescent is the best light source is that we grew up under it. This preference might not be as strong today as it once was because more people have spent their formative years under blue light from television and fluorescent sources. People do look "better" when lighted with incandescent than with other sources, but its usefulness for general lighting is declining rapidly because of its inefficient conversion of electricity to light.

About 85 percent of the radiant energy produced by incandescent lamps is heat in the infrared form. The reduced radiant heat per footcandle is one of the main reasons light levels increased so dramatically when fluorescent came along in the 1940s.

Incandescent lamps are at the low end of the efficiency ladder of sources (see Figure 4.21). A 7-watt night-light produces only about 7 lumens for each watt used, while the highest wattage incandescent currently produced (10,000) exceeds 30 lumens per watt (LPW). Common household bulbs of 60 to 150 watts are in the 15 to 20 LPW range. These examples correctly indicate that the higher the wattage, the higher the efficiency. One 100-watt lamp, for instance, produces more light than two 60s. This relationship is true for all lamp families.

Another important effect on efficiency is the life designed into the filament. Like an almost inflexible seesaw, efficiency goes down as life is increased and vice-versa. A 60-watt lamp designed for 10 hours of service produces 17 times as much light as the same fila-

15

ment designed to last a million hours. There is no magic involved
with long-life filaments, just designing them with different lengths
and diameters so they will burn cooler than the shorter-life variety.
Manufacturing tolerances on filament life, as shown in Figure 4.1,
and other design features such as light output and wattage are extremely tight as a result of experience gained from the millions produced since Edison's invention in 1879. Life tolerances are well illustrated by automotive headlights. Often the second light will fail
while the user is still getting around to replacing the first burnout.
When the first bulb burns out in a new chandelier, stand by for the
rest of them to fail in a short time.

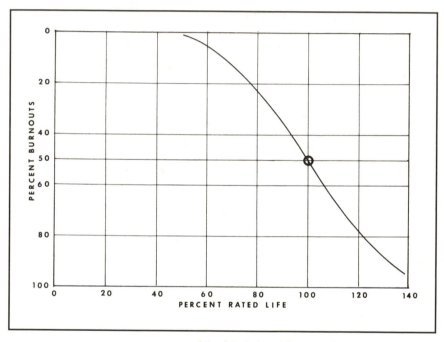

4.1. A typical mortality curve for a large quantity of high-volume
lamps, such as common household bulbs. Note that 100 percent
rated life is the point when 50 percent of the lamps have already
burned out and also the sharp increase in number of failures as rated
life is approached. (*Courtesy of the General Electric Company*)

Common practice in commercial and industrial buildings is to
buy lamps designed for 130 volts and operate them on 120-volt circuits. This apparently minor change in applied voltage causes them
to last three times as many hours as their ratings, but they produce
only 75 percent of their rated light output. Often such users find that
they have to step up to the next wattage to get the light they need. As

detailed in Chapter 8, they are thus not getting the bargain they think they are.

Since electricity is far and away the highest cost of operating any lighting system, long-life, low-efficiency incandescent lamps make economic sense only when labor cost for replacement is extremely high, such as in stairwells and on water towers. As electrical costs continue to rise, long-life lamps are going to be even less logical. Operating cost relationships are fully discussed in Chapter 8.

An extremely short life will, of course, result in inordinate costs for lamps and the labor to change them. A compromise at 750 or 1000 hours has been reached for most applications. If economy alone is considered, an even shorter life design for homes is indicated, but many people would rebel at the bother of buying and changing even more bulbs than they do now.

Another effect on filament efficiency, besides life design and wattage, is designed voltage. Household lamps made to be operated on 120 volts do not produce as much light per watt as comparable 12-volt automotive lamps. A whole family of 12-volt lamps called MR-16 is currently in wide use for display lighting in stores, museums, and the like, not only for this higher efficiency but also because low-voltage filaments are smaller and allow better beam control.

As all lamps, incandescents decrease in light output over life. The explanation is that little particles of tungsten are literally boiled off the filament as they burn and collect on the nearest cool spot. In gas-filled lamps of about 40 watts or higher, that cool spot is on the glass bulb directly above the filament. The absence of a gas current in vacuum lamps causes tungsten to deposit evenly all over the bulb. In each case, the resultant darkening absorbs light and lessens output.

As the filament loses tungsten (used because of its high melting temperature) by the evaporation described above, it gets thinner at some spots than others. These points get hotter than the rest of the filament, boil off particles faster, and eventually one of them gets hot enough to melt the filament completely, thus ending the life of the lamp. Often such failures will occur when the lamp is turned on because of a small surge of electricity from the switching process, but it would have failed anyway after just a few more minutes of operation during its previous use.

Bases, some of which are shown in Figure 4.2, are required on all lamps to conduct electricity in and out, and (on most) to hold them in place mechanically. The exact style is dependent on intended use. The familiar screw bases, small for low wattages and large for

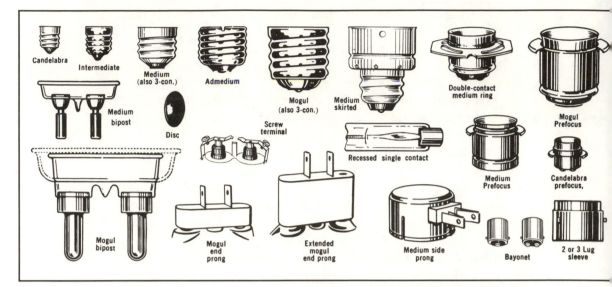

4.2. The lamp bases shown are those most frequently encountered (not drawn to scale). For application refer to the text, Appendix, or manufacturers' catalogs. (*Courtesy of the General Electric Company*)

high, are used in most applications. Bayonet bases, with one or two contacts on the bottom, are used in cars, airplanes, and other such locations where vibration might loosen a screw base. Whenever an optical system requires the filament to be in exactly the same position each time a new lamp is installed, a prefocus or some kind of pin base is used.

The glass bulb (described in the trade by letter as shown in Figure 4.3 and by maximum diameter in eighths of an inch) can be clear or frosted or have a white finish, as illustrated in Figure 4.4. The frosted and white finishes are used to decrease annoying filament brightness and soften shadows. Bulbs are also colored for decorative effects.

Reflector (R) lamps, produced by coating the interior surface of parabolic or elliptical bulbs with silver or aluminum, are very useful in any lighting design. While beam control is not extremely tight, all the light does go out in one general direction. They sometimes break if water falls on them (hence the name "indoor flood"), but they are cheaper than the PAR lamps described below. Different beam patterns are obtained by changing the diffusion on the face. Reflector lamps are also made in various colors.

PAR lamps (you are really accepted in lighting circles if you know that PAR stands for parabolic aluminized reflector), shown with some of the many R sizes in Figure 4.5, are made of so-called

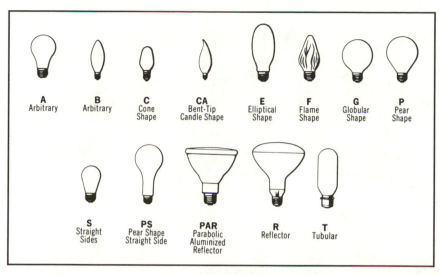

4.3. Bulb shapes are designated by letter as shown and size (diameter) in eighths of an inch. Only incandescent lamps are shown, but the same system is used for all lamp types. (*Courtesy of the General Electric Company*)

4.4. A and PS bulbs are available in clear, inside frost, and white finishes. Colors can also be applied to get desired effects. (*Courtesy of the General Electric Company*)

hard glass, resistant to breakage by water (hence "outdoor flood"), and available in a great variety of wattages, colors, beam spreads, sizes, and voltages. Any application requiring a tight beam should use PAR rather than R lamps.

Listed lumen output for an R or PAR lamp will be considerably

4.5. PAR and R lamps are made in a variety of sizes, wattages, beam patterns, and colors. See the Appendix or manufacturers' catalogs for other types. (*Courtesy of the General Electric Company*)

less than that for a comparable general service lamp with the same designed wattage, life, and voltage because light is lost inside the lamp itself. Lumen comparisons with R or PAR lamps should be made with the photometric data of fixtures after raw lamp lumens have been processed into beams.

Several low-voltage (5.5- and 12-volt) PAR lamps have a hemispherical reflector over the filament (Figure 4.6), which prevents light from escaping the lamp at wide uncontrolled angles. Such filament covers in low-beam headlights are the reason for the sharp beam cutoff just below the oncoming driver's eyes. These narrowbeam, low-voltage lamps are useful for projecting light along columns, highlighting small items, and the like.

Tables available from both lamp and fixture manufacturers, showing beam patterns for R and PAR lamps, are indispensable for achieving accurate lighting designs. Figure 4.7 shows candlepower curves for some common lamps. Use of these curves with the inverse square law (see Chapter 9) allows the lighting designer to accurately forecast brightnesses at crucial points in the space. The candlepower at 0 degrees from the beam axis in Figure 4.7 is that brightness observed when looking directly at the face of the lamp.

Since only half the total beam is shown in most candlepower curves, a description of 30-degree beam spread really means twice that when the full beam is considered. Calculating the area covered

4.6. The filament shield shown on this 12-volt PAR lamp directs light back into the accurately designed reflector and thence lens so it can be formed into a small, tight beam. (*Courtesy of the General Electric Company*)

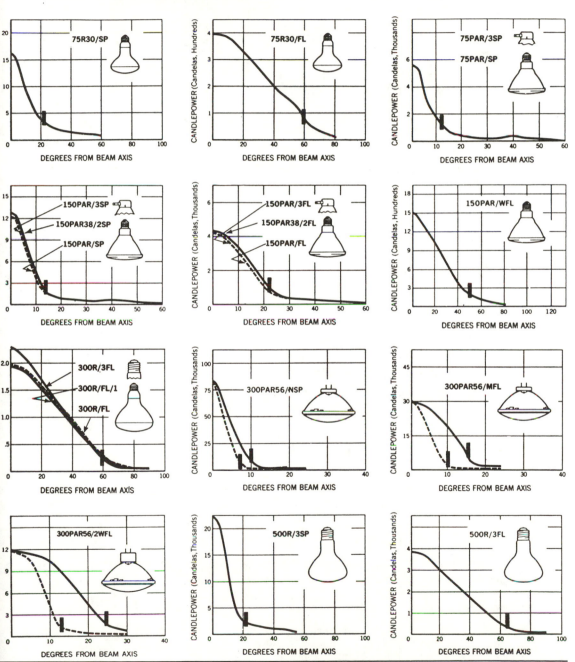

4.7. Candlepower distribution curves for some common R and PAR lamps. Candlepower data obtained from such curves are used with the inverse square law to obtain light levels at a point. The vertical mark part way down each curve indicates the nominal limit of the beam, which is usually 10 percent of maximum candlepower. Note that only half the full pattern is used. (*Courtesy of the General Electric Company*)

at various distances by a given lamp requires some mathematical knowledge, but fortunately manufacturers have done that work for us. Figures 4.8 and 4.9 are examples of such aids.

Approximate Initial Footcandle Patterns

150-WATT PAR-38 FLOOD aiming angle 0°, H=10 feet   aiming angle 30°, H=10 feet

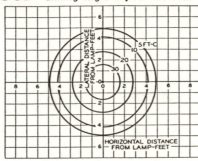

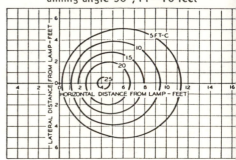

150-WATT R-40 FLOOD   aiming angle 0°, H=10 feet   aiming angle 30°, H=10 feet
(Also 300 and 500 Watts)

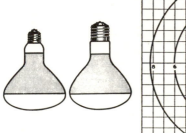

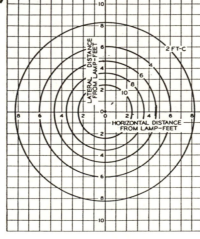

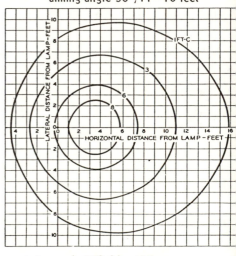

150-WATT PAR-38 SPOT aiming angle 0°, H=10 feet   aiming angle 30°, H=10 feet

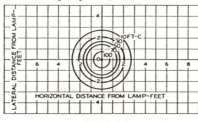

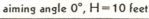

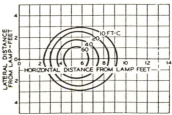

150-WATT R-40 SPOT   aiming angle 0°, H=10 feet   aiming angle 30°, H=10 feet
(Also 300 and 500 Watts)

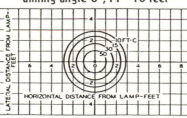

Footcandles and area coverage for common 150-watt R and R lamps at various aiming angles. Similar data for higher wattage R lamps are shown in Figure 4.9. (*Courtesy of the General Electric Company*)

aiming angle 45°, H = 10 feet

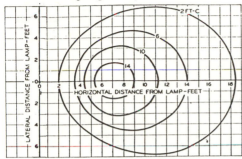

aiming angle 45°, H = 10 feet

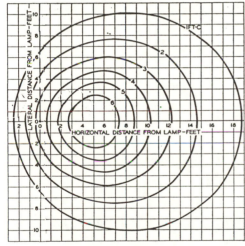

FOR OTHER WATTAGES AND MOUNTING DISTANCES

When using the footcandle patterns or footcandle profiles for other mounting distances (H) than the ones shown, multiply the distance and footcandle values shown on the patterns by the appropriate factor below. For 300- and 500-watt R-40 lamps, use the curves for the 150-watt lamps, and multiply footcandles by the factors shown.

For This Lamp . . .	At This Mounting Height . . .	Multiply Distances By . . .	And Multiply Footcandles By . . .
150-w. PAR-38 150-w. R-40 Spots & Floods	5 7.5 10 15 20	.5 .75 1.0 1.5 2.0	4.0 1.8 1.0 .45 .25
300-w. R-40 Spot & Flood (use patterns for 150-watt lamps)	5 7.5 10 15 20	.5 .75 1.0 1.5 2.0	8.0 3.6 2.0 .90 .50
500-w. R-40 Spot & Flood (use patterns for 150-watt lamps)	10 15 20 25	1.0 1.5 2.0 2.5	3.2 1.44 .80 .51
200-w. PAR-46 300-w. PAR-56 Spot & Flood	15 20 25 30 35 40	.75 1.0 1.25 1.5 1.75 2.0	1.8 1.0 .64 .45 .33 .25

aiming angle 45°, H = 10 feet

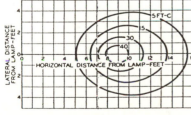

aiming angle 60°, H = 10 feet

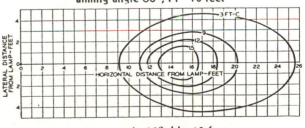

aiming angle 45°, H = 10 feet

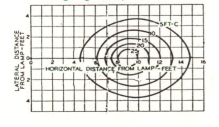

aiming angle 60°, H = 10 feet

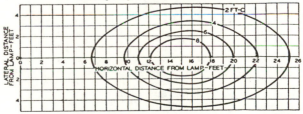

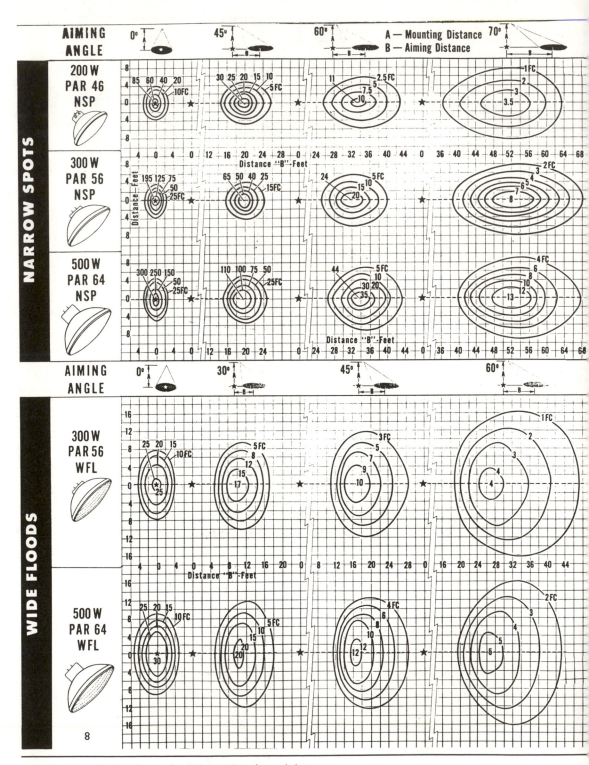

4.9. Diagrams showing footcandle patterns at various aiming angles for the higher wattage PAR lamps. Note that the mounting height used in each table is 20 feet. Such charts for other lamps, mounting distances, and aiming angles are available from fixture and lamp manufacturers. (*Courtesy of the General Electric Company*)

Three-way lamps, handy for changing light levels as activities change, are constructed with two filaments connected as shown in Figure 4.10. Lamp manufacturers design the low-wattage filament for longer life than that of the high-wattage one to recognize the fact that it will burn more of the time. Since they are used different lengths of time and because of manufacturing tolerances, one of the filaments in a three-way bulb will always burn out before the other.

Rough-service lamps, often mistakenly chosen in an attempt to get long life, have extra filament supports for mechanical strength. Since each added filament support decreases light output, such

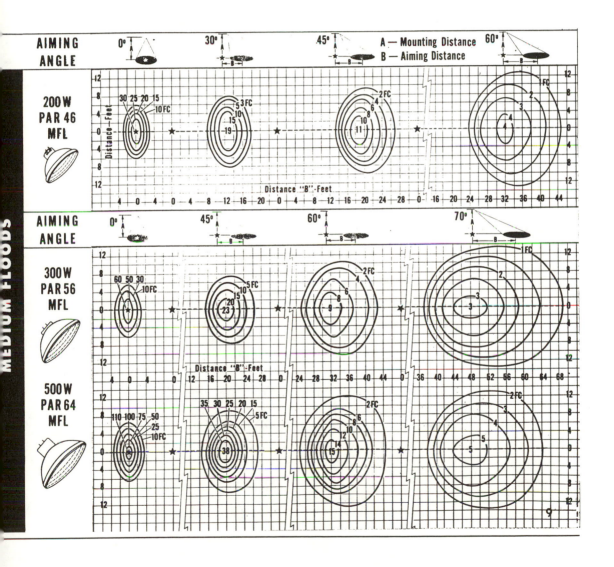

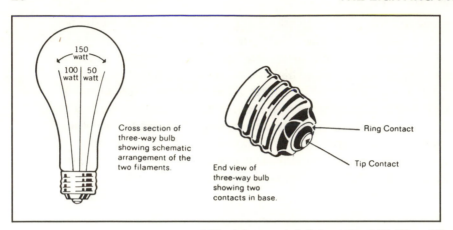

150 watt

100 watt | 50 watt

Cross section of three-way bulb showing schematic arrangement of the two filaments.

End view of three-way bulb showing two contacts in base.

Ring Contact

Tip Contact

4.10. A three-way bulb that operates at 50, 100, or 150 watts dependent on switch position. The switch connects the tip, ring, or base shell contacts in different combinations to activate the proper filament or filaments. (*Courtesy of the General Electric Company*)

lamps should be used only on the end of a drop cord or other such rough-use application. Vibration service lamps are, as the name implies, designed to hold up when subjected to prolonged vibration.

Infrared heat lamps, most often seen in the red-ended reflector variety, are merely incandescent lamps designed for extremely long lives. The red face on household heat lamps is there only to reduce brightness and to make it look like a heat lamp. Clear lamps are cheaper and do exactly the same warming job. Since 80 to 90 percent of radiation from any incandescent lamp is infrared, ordinary lighting lamps can be used for the same purposes as those designated "heat" or "infrared."

Another type of infrared lamp uses a tubular quartz bulb only $3/8$ of an inch in diameter and thus is called a "quartz heat lamp." Quartz, a very pure form of glass, is used because it melts at a higher temperature than ordinary glass. These lamps are useful when the application calls for the smallest possible fixture or the greatest concentration of energy.

An extension of the quartz heat lamp is the quartz lighting lamp, known variously as "quartz halogen," "quartz iodine," "quartz," or a trade name. Figure 4.11 indicates the chemical cycle inside the lamp that results in almost no loss of light over its life, while Figure 4.12 shows resultant blackening if no halogen gas is used. This more constant light output, plus its small size and slightly whiter color compared to other incandescents, has given quartz a somewhat mystical, almost magical aura. Smaller, cheaper fixtures

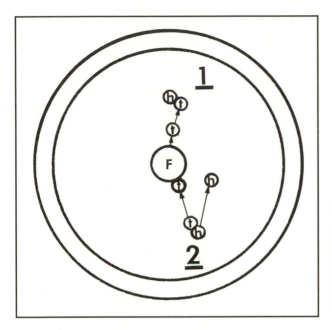

4.11. The halogen cycle starts with the chemical formation of a gas by the combination of tungsten particles boiled off the filament and a halogen gas, either bromine or iodine. Formed a short distance away from the filament, this gas circulates inside the lamp until it reaches a certain high temperature, at which point the tungsten and halogen separate and the tungsten deposits back on the filament or one of the support wires.

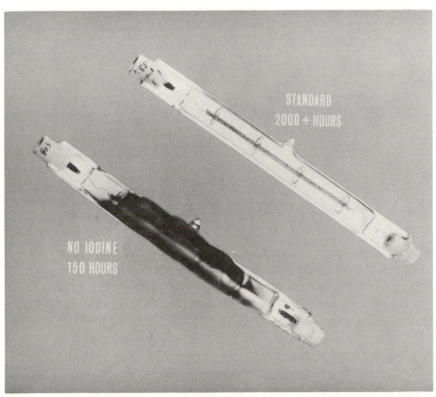

4.12. Absence of iodine (or bromine) gas in the lower bulb allows dense blackening to occur after just a few burning hours, while the clean lamp at the top results from the chemical action indicated in Figure 4.11. (*Courtesy of the General Electric Company*)

than those required by standard incandescent lamps find wide application in stage, studio, sports, and display areas where well-defined beams of light are important. An additional feature is that designed life of quartz is longer than comparable standard lamps. The recent application of an infrared-reflecting coating to the bulb of linear quartz lamps (Figure 4.12) has resulted in greatly increased efficiency for some types.

Quartz filament tubes have been successfully used in PAR bulbs and (most recently, for general lighting applications) in a family of types known as MR-16. The name stems from "mirrored reflector" and its most common diameter, 2 ($^{16}/_8$) inches. These low-voltage display lamps have found wide use for display lighting because of low-wattage, small fixtures, excellent beam control, and slightly whiter light than comparable PAR or R lamps. Their size relative to PAR lamps is illustrated in Figure 4.13.

4.13. The lamps shown, from left to right, are a standard 150-watt, PAR38 spot; an energy-saving 120-watt, PAR38 spot; a 50-watt, 12-volt PAR36 featuring a filament cover that allows a very small beam spread; and a 50-watt, 12-volt MR-16 quartz halogen lamp. (*Courtesy of the General Electric Company*)

One advantage incandescent has over other sources is minimal fixture requirements. All that is really needed is a socket. This results in low cost per fixture, but not necessarily low cost per footcandle, because so many more watts are required with incandescent to reach a desired light level than if more efficient sources are used.

Other important advantages of incandescent not matched by any other source are color and a small size that allows accurate light beams. Fixtures can be designed to produce small, large, round, or square beam patterns—almost any shape or size desired. Light output from many fixtures can be changed by changing wattage. If 75-watt bulbs produce too much light, simply change to 60-watt ones.

The major, very important disadvantage of incandescent lamps is that they do not produce much light per watt. Another, already mentioned, is the high percentage of infrared in their output. This radiant heat can be impossible to compensate for with air conditioning at light levels above about 40 footcandles. (Incandescent characteristics are compared with other sources in Figure 4.9.)

FLUORESCENT

Fluorescent lamps do not produce light the way incandescents do. There is no wire running the length of the tube, only cathodes at each end and gas, mostly mercury, filling the tube. The cathodes act alternatively as emitters and collectors of electrons and thus form an arc, similar to lightning, through the gas. The arc itself produces very little light but a lot of radiation at 253.7 nanometers in the far ultraviolet portion of the spectrum. A phosphor coating the inside of the bulb converts that ultraviolet to light. Almost limitless nuances of color renditions, described in Table 4.1, are possible by varying proportions of different phosphor formulas. The only way to choose a light source for its color is to see it demonstrated.

TABLE 4.1. A simplified chart for color choice of fluorescent lamps

Name	Efficiency	Colors enhanced	Colors dimmed	Comments
Cool white (CW)	High	Blue, green	Red, orange	Most common
Light white (LW)	High	Blue, green	Red, orange	Matches CW
Cool white deluxe (CWX)	Low	All	None	Fairest to all colors
SP41, color 74	High	Blue, green	Red, orange	Better color than CW and LW
SPX 41, color 84	High	Blue, green	Red, orange	Better color than SP41 and color 74
SP35	High	Red, orange	Green	Compromise between warm and cool sources
SPX 35	High	Red, orange	Green	Better color than SP35
Warm white (WW)	High	Yellow, orange	Blue, red	Often used for a warm atmosphere
Warm white deluxe (WWX)	Low	Red, orange	Blue, green	Flattering to skin. Close to incandescent
SP30, color 73	High	Red, orange	Blue, green	Efficient WWX
SPX 30, color 83	High	Red, orange	Blue, green	Best for stores
C50, Vitalite	Low	All	None	Bluish CWX
Plant light	Low	Blue, red	Green, yellow	Flattering to some flowers

Many other colors are available, some with highly touted, even miraculous sounding properties, but the ones listed in Table 4.1 are adequate for most lighting palettes. (A color comparison with other sources is indicated in Figure 4.20.) Two other fluorescent colors deserve some attention. White, one of the first phosphors produced, remains a highly efficient and satisfactory color-rendering source. It is midway in color appearance between the bluish cool white and the rather yellowish warm white. Another early color, daylight, produces almost no red and a lot of blue, is low in light output, and costs more than many other colors. For these reasons, daylight fluorescent color should be used only in the design of plastic signs. Nonetheless, some employers in the South continue to use it as a sort of subliminal air conditioning.

Fluorescent lamps are about five times as efficient as incandescent lamps at converting electricity, but only about 20 percent of the input watts emerge as light. Reference to Table A.11 in the Appendix and Figure 4.21 shows that, like incandescent lamps, high-wattage fluorescent lamps produce more lumens per watt than lower-wattage ones. Also, phosphors that have high color-rendering properties are usually not as efficient as others such as cool white, warm white, and light white. There are some newer lamp colors (shown in Table 4.1 and the fluorescent tables in the Appendix) that provide both good color rendering and high light output.

As other types, fluorescent lamps have one or two bases (Figure 4.14) to provide a path for electricity and to hold the lamp in place.

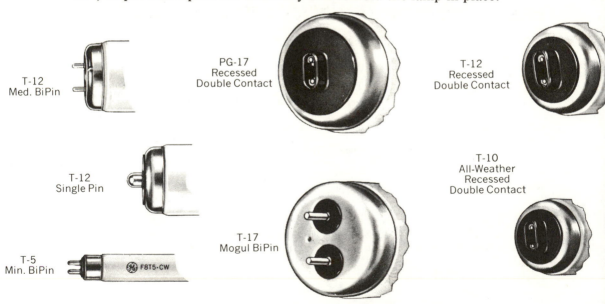

T-12
Med. BiPin

PG-17
Recessed
Double Contact

T-12
Recessed
Double Contact

T-12
Single Pin

T-10
All-Weather
Recessed
Double Contact

T-5
Min. BiPin

T-17
Mogul BiPin

4.14.   Common fluorescent lamp bases. The most common are medium bipin used on the popular 40-watt lamps and single pin used on the so-called "slimline." (*Courtesy of the General Electric Company*)

The cathodes in fluorescent lamps consist of coiled tungsten wire with a chemical powder, called emission mix, deposited on them. Emission mix is constantly being driven off the cathodes as the lamp burns, forming dark rings on the bulb; when it is all gone, the lamp dies.

Not all fluorescent lamps are made in straight tubes. There are several varieties of U shapes, some of which are shown in Figures 4.15 and 4.16. There are circular lamps in four sizes, called circline, and a growing variety of H, W, and other shapes. Some of these may

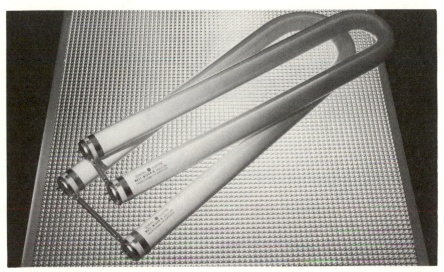

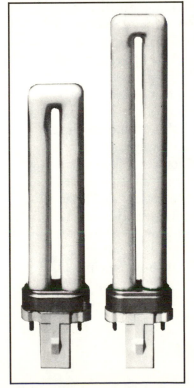

4.15. These U-shaped lamps in two leg spacings and many colors were developed for use in the 2- by 2-foot fixtures spawned by the 5-foot module. See Chapter 13 for a discussion. (*Courtesy of the General Electric Company*)

4.16. These compact fluorescent lamps were developed as an alternative to incandescent. Many are marketed as a kit complete with ballast and medium screw base as a direct replacement in existing fixtures. (*Courtesy of the General Electric Company*)

stay around, but caution is advised until they come into wider use. The leading edge of lamp technology is sometimes nicked.

Discharge lamps, including fluorescent, that operate by an electric arc through a gas require devices called ballasts to limit current flow. Without a ballast in the circuit, the lamp would draw an increasing amount of current until it self-destructed. Some ballasts serve the secondary purpose of providing voltage high enough to start the lamp. Ballasts (Figure 4.17) usually remain unseen inside the fixture.

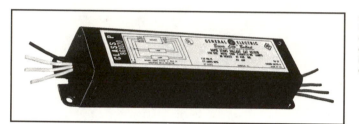

4.17. The ballast shown here provides proper electrical values to operate one or more fluorescent lamps. (*Courtesy of the General Electric Company*)

There is always ballast hum from a fluorescent lighting system, but the noise is usually masked by other sounds in the space—air movement, conversation, typewriters, street traffic, and the like. An industry tale has it that ballasts hum because they can't remember the words, but it is really because of steel laminations inside them vibrating to 60-hertz (cycles per second) current. Manufacturers have recognized this noise by assigning sound ratings to their ballasts, from A to E, with A being the quietest. Since there is no industry standard for this scale, however, each manufacturer has its own testing method. Ballasts at or near the end of life sometimes announce themselves by becoming very loud.

While sound ratings are not standardized, other ballast classifications are. Class P means they contain a temperature-sensing device for overheating protection, ETL (Electrical Testing Laboratories) and UL (Underwriters Laboratories) labels mean they are safe, and a certification by CBM (Certified Ballast Manufacturers) shows that the lamps will deliver 95 percent of rated light output under specified conditions. Non-CBM ballasts can drive lamps at as low as 50 percent of rating, with disastrous results on planned lighting levels. Temperature rating for a ballast, usually 50, 20, 0, or −20 degrees Fahrenheit, shows only the temperature at which the ballast will start the lamp. It gives absolutely no indication of how much light the lamp will deliver at those temperatures. Variations in light output due to temperature differences are discussed later in this chapter.

Besides the audible noise mentioned above, fluorescent systems also generate radio interference. The radiation can come from the lamp itself or the wires carrying electricity to the fixture, or it can be fed directly back through the circuits to other devices. A valuable test for sensitivity of the audio circuit of a radio, in fact, is to hold it near a fluorescent fixture to see if it can amplify the signal. Electronic filters and conductive lenses can be installed in the fixture to eliminate such interference.

There are several circuits, or electrical systems, used to operate fluorescent lamps. First developed was the preheat or starter circuit, still in wide use for short lamps such as those in desk lamps and appliances. This method employs either a momentary-hold switch or a glow-switch starter to heat up the cathodes before the arc is struck through the lamp. Preheat circuits are almost obsolete for general lighting applications because of fixture costs, still-unreliable starters, and annoying blinking when the lamp starts.

Next came the instant-start circuit featuring a ballast that provides voltage high enough to strike an arc through the lamp without any preheating current. The lamp lights instantly, has only one contact at each end, and no starting device is needed. The so-called slimline lamps, usually 8 feet long and seen extensively in bare-lamp store installations, use this starting system. A disadvantage of instant-start circuits is that the ballasts are relatively large, expensive, and inefficient. An offshoot of instant-start circuits called trigger-start is in wide use for residential fixtures. It provides instantaneous light but has the unpleasant side effect of shortening lamp life.

The rapid-start circuit, far and away the most popular operating system for general lighting, uses no separate starting device and provides some light immediately, with full light output in about a second. Rapid-start lamps can be dimmed by using the proper equipment, but the required ballasts, auxiliaries, and controls are quite expensive. Such costs should decrease as solid state (electronic) ballasts are improved.

Electronic ballasts for fluorescent lamps burst onto the lighting scene in great profusion during and after the oil embargo in the 1970s. Since ballasts are merely current-limiting and sometimes voltage-increasing devices, it occurred to electronic engineers all over the world that they could design better ballasts to replace the inefficient, noisy, and heavy ones currently in use and thus save a lot of energy. It was easy to design them to operate lamps at several thousand hertz, thus making them more efficient. The ballasts themselves would have fewer losses, and dimming would be easier than the rather cumbersome method then in use. The problem to date has been unreliability caused by the high number of parts required. Some early models exceeded 100 separate pieces — resistors, transistors, capacitors, and such — failure of any one of which could incapacitate the ballast. The future of electronic ballasts is unknown at this writing.

As previously mentioned, a singular characteristic of fluorescent lamps is that each lamp type peaks in light output and wattage at a certain temperature, and both decrease when either hotter or colder. For this reason standard fluorescents should not be used outdoors without special precautions. Peak light output for the common 40-watt and slimline lamps is at normal indoor temperatures, while some so-called outdoor lamps give maximum light at −20 degrees Fahrenheit.

Another difference from other sources is that fluorescent lamp lives are shortened by on-off operation. The first hour of burning uses up the life-controlling emission mix faster than later burning time. Companies using large numbers of fluorescent lamps are aware of this attribute and sometimes determine a break-even time to turn them off or let them burn when not needed. The added costs of turning them off are more lamps and labor to change them, while additional electricity is used when they are left on. In recent years that break-even point has decreased to about five minutes, and most major users are treating them just like incandescent — turning them off when not needed.

"Nominal" length of a fluorescent lamp does not refer to the actual length of the lamp but to the space into which a minimal fixture will fit. If you have a 24-inch space, you can fit a "24-inch" lamp into it, including lampholders.

A common folk fear in this country is that an encounter with a broken fluorescent lamp is tantamount to instant death of some mysterious nature. This fear was even exploited in a soap opera showing a gorilla in imminent danger because it broke a fluorescent lamp inside its cage. Trash collectors have been known to leave fluorescent lamps alongside the curb for weeks because of irrational fear.

The facts behind this fluorescent fable are that in 1949 or thereabouts a worker at a lamp plant became ill, was hospitalized, and died, all without successful diagnosis by the attendant physicians. The eventual conclusion was that he died of beryllium poisoning, which was traced to his job of breaking up fluorescent lamps in a small room. At that time, but not since, beryllium was used in the phosphor of one color of fluorescent lamp. The medical case was written up, published in at least one national periodical, and has been reprinted from time to time since then. No such publicity has ever been given the fact that the industry quit using that phosphor as soon as it was even suspect.

The relatively large size of fluorescents can be both an advantage and a disadvantage. An advantage is that they are a low-brightness, thus visually comfortable, source. The linear form is perfect for lighted valances, coves, and such. Light is hard to control from large sources, however, since huge reflectors would be required to obtain any sort of a well-defined beam pattern; thus, despite their high LPW rating, fluorescent lamps are not used in such applications as spotlighting and street lighting.

A major disadvantage of discharge lamps, including fluorescent, is that wattages cannot be interchanged in the same fixture without installing a different ballast. Once a fixture is installed, wattage is set except for minor changes with energy-saving lamps.

HIGH-INTENSITY DISCHARGE

The family of lamps known as high-intensity discharge, mercifully shortened to HID, includes mercury, metal halide, and high-pressure sodium. Another source, low-pressure sodium, is not technically part of this grouping but is often included in comparisons. Figure 4.18 shows all three types.

All HID lamps produce light by a process best described as "lighting in a bottle." An electric current flows through a conducting gas, as with fluorescent lamps, but unlike that lamp the arc itself is the main light source. Phosphor can be added to the outer jacket (bulb) to change color characteristics, but most of the light comes directly from the arc. The arc tube—as the glass, quartz, or ceramic bottle containing the gas is called—has a cathode at each end to conduct electricity in and out. Other wires and devices are required inside the outer jacket to operate the lamp and, as for others, a base outside provides an electrical circuit and holds the lamp in place.

The outer jacket is required not only to hold color-altering phosphor but also to keep air away from the metal parts. On mercury and metal halide lamps it serves the additional function of blocking harmful ultraviolet radiation emitted by the arc tube. High-pressure sodium generates no such ultraviolet.

Like fluorescent, HID lamps also require a ballast to limit current and provide voltage high enough to start the lamp.

4.18. Shown from left to right are metal halide, mercury, and high-pressure sodium lamps. Mercury and metal halide lamps may have phosphor added to the outer jacket to change colors. (*Courtesy of the General Electric Company*)

MERCURY

Mercury lamps, the oldest of the HID group, are made in wattages from 40 to 1000, have an initial efficiency of about 50 lumens per watt (less when ballast losses are included), and have an extremely long life. The current life rating is 24,000 + hours, but in-service life is probably twice that. All this would be great if the light output stayed high, but, as with all lamps, it decreases. Many of the mercury lamps still burning are producing less than one-third of their original light. (See Figure 4.21 and Table A.3 in the Appendix for more exact data.)

Clear mercury (without phosphor) produces only blue and green light and is useless for most applications. After some evolution over the years, the current cool and warm phosphors are acceptable for many commercial areas. Because of mercury's low efficiency and poor lumen maintenance, however, other sources can usually do a better job. Mercury lamps, except the low-wattage ones, are considered obsolete light sources.

There are some mercury lamps (called self-ballasted) containing internal ballasts that can directly replace incandescent lamps. Compared to incandescent, they have longer lives and slightly higher efficiencies, but their prices are so high that it is usually cheaper to install new fixtures using standard HID lamps and ballasts.

METAL HALIDE

Metal halide lamps, currently made in wattages up to 1500, are quite simply pepped-up mercury lamps. Metallic halides added to the arc tubes cause them to produce about 50 percent more lumens per watt and much better color rendition than mercury lamps. They are harder to start, so that different, more expensive ballasts are normally required; they cost more and are shorter lived than mercury, but the higher efficiency usually offsets these shortcomings. See Chapter 8 for a discussion of the reasons.

The color of clear metal halide lamps has proved fully acceptable for use in stores, offices, and other commercial establishments. The phosphor-coated variety is warmer and has optical advantages in certain fixtures. An even warmer version, commonly called 3K for its color temperature (3000 degrees Kelvin), is being used more and more extensively in merchandising. The 1500-watt metal halide lamp is the predominant choice for outdoor sports applications because of excellent color rendition and the small arc tube that allows good beam control.

HIGH-PRESSURE SODIUM

High-pressure sodium lamps, as the name implies, contain sodium along with other ingredients to aid operation. They have a wide wattage range, from 35 to 1000, and the highest efficiency of any source that can even remotely be considered white—golden white perhaps but white, nonetheless. It has been known for years that sodium lamps are very efficient, but until 1965 when a suitable synthetic ceramic was produced, there was no bottle that could hold the highly volatile chemical at relatively high pressures. While the color rendition of high-pressure sodium is not suitable for merchandising, it has been used successfully in the public areas of shopping malls, public buildings, and the like, and is certainly fine for almost all industrial, warehousing, and outdoor applications. Experiments in offices (Figure 13.3) have proved less than spectacular. High-pressure sodium exhibits very high efficiency, long life (24,000+ hours), and good lumen maintenance. All these benefits convert to low-cost lighting installations and explain why there are so many high-pressure sodium installations around.

Mercury lamps fail for the same reason fluorescents do—the emission mix on the cathodes is used up; but metal halide and high-pressure sodium can be different. The various materials in metal halide lamps form a rather unstable mixture inside the arc tube, which during operation can react chemically with the quartz of the arc tube, leak out, and thus cause lamp failure. High-pressure sodium lamps can fail in a similar manner, with sodium leaking out, and also by increasing in voltage during their life to the point that the ballast cannot sustain the arc. When this happens the high-pressure sodium lamp will light, operate for a short time, go off, then relight again. This condition is known as cycling. Whatever their failure mode, HID lamps have a long life and are thus tempting for many applications.

LOW-PRESSURE SODIUM

Low-pressure sodium lamps, long popular in Europe for street and highway lighting, virtually disappeared in this country during the fifties and were revived when the oil embargo struck in the seventies. The renewed interest was due to its high efficiency (180 lumens per watt), but that number alone does not tell the complete story. It is a monochromatic source, meaning it emits only one color, yellow, so that anything seen under it will look either yellow or a shade of gray. It is a large source, the 180-watt version being 4 feet long, optically like fluorescent, thus impossible to form into a well-defined beam. This characteristic, along with its hideous color and special disposal methods, make low-pressure sodium suitable only for limited applications.

SUMMARY

There is no magic light source. Designers (who tend to use nothing but incandescent) and engineers (who may be preoccupied with costs and thus end up with fluorescent or HID) are both wrong if they do not consider alternative lamps when the needs of the space so dictate. Figure 4.19 is a starting reference for lamp choice. At least one of the parameters listed is usually most important to the lighting designer, for example, the color-rendering index and initial cost in an art gallery. Not all the advantages and disadvantages are listed. Incandescent, for example, with all its life and efficiency problems, is often chosen because of color, ease of dimming, or the precise beam control possible with that small source.

CHARACTERISTIC →	Color-Rendering Index			Initial Efficiency (LPW)			Lumen Maintenance			Rated Average Life			Initial Cost			Operating Cost (Equal Light)		
RELATIVE LAMP RATING →	High	Medium	Low	High	Medium	Low	High	Medium	Low	Long	Medium	Short	High	Medium	Low	High	Medium	Low
INCANDESCENT and QUARTZ	X					X	X					X			X	X		
FLUORESCENT (CW, WW, LW)		X		X			X				X			X				X
FLUORESCENT (CWX, WWX)	X				X		X				X		X				X	
MERCURY (DX, WDX)		X			X				X	X				X			X	
METAL HALIDE	X			X			X				X		X					X
HIGH-PRESSURE SODIUM			X	X			X			X				X				X

4.19. This light source selector indicates in broad ranges the relative attributes of source families. The two cost columns, "initial" and "operating," are based on equal maintained footcandles rather than fixture price, and the fluorescent groupings list only a few of the many colors available.

It should be noted in Figure 4.19 that good color rendition is usually traded for some other desirable characteristic such as efficiency or life. Lamps with poor color rendition usually have the lowest operating cost. Figure 4.21 shows efficiencies and lives of most widely used lamps, while Figures 4.20 and 4.22 are two different color representations.

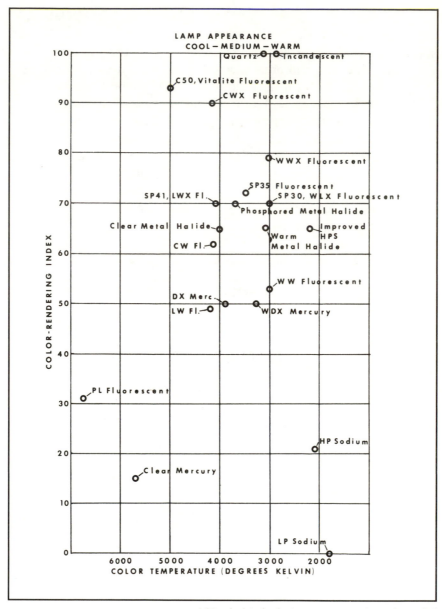

LAMP APPEARANCE
COOL — MEDIUM — WARM

Quartz — Incandescent

C50, Vitalite Fluorescent

CWX Fluorescent

WWX Fluorescent

SP35 Fluorescent

SP41, LWX Fl. SP30, WLX Fluorescent

Phosphored Metal Halide

Clear Metal Halide Improved HPS

CW Fl. Warm Metal Halide

WW Fluorescent

DX Merc.

LW Fl. WDX Mercury

PL Fluorescent

HP Sodium

Clear Mercury

LP Sodium

COLOR-RENDERING INDEX

COLOR TEMPERATURE (DEGREES KELVIN)

4.20. A plot of color temperatures against color-rendering indexes for a number of lamps. As explained in Chapter 3, the higher the color temperature, the bluer the light source.

40

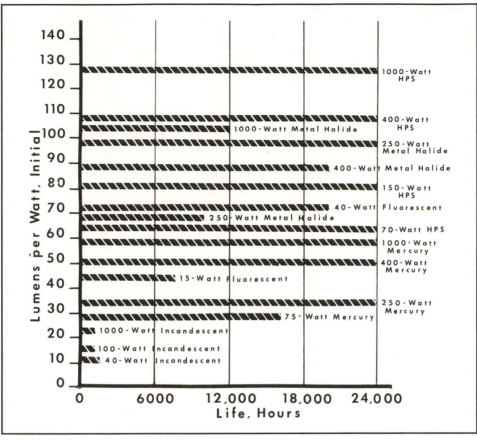

4.21. This chart shows efficiency versus life for a variety of lamps and clearly indicates the reason for choosing the highest suitable wattage within a source family.

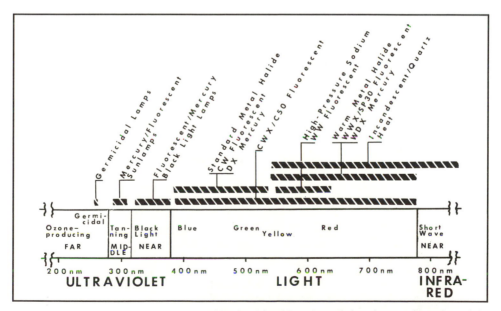

4.22. A quick guide to lamp choice when certain portions of the spectrum are desired. Cool colors are emphasized by metal halide, cool white fluorescent, and deluxe mercury, for example. Cool white deluxe and C50 fluorescent are considered fairest to all colors.

5

CONTROL OF LIGHT

LIGHT IS CONTROLLED in lighting applications by reflection, transmission, refraction, absorption, polarization, and concealment. Figure 5.1 illustrates details. All fixtures except bare sockets use one or more of these methods.

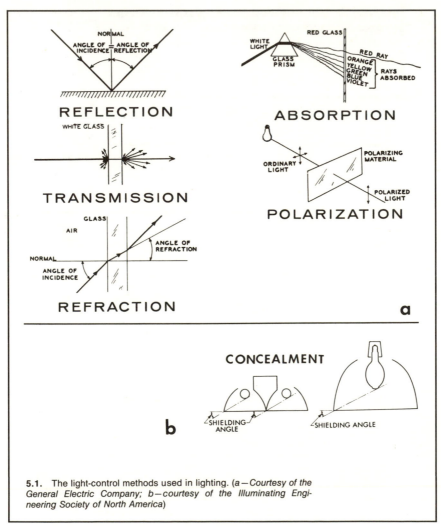

5.1.   The light-control methods used in lighting. (*a — Courtesy of the General Electric Company; b — courtesy of the Illuminating Engineering Society of North America*)

REFLECTION

Reflection from a surface can be at the same angle from which it strikes (as a mirror or glossy magazine), at many angles (as a matte blotter or newsprint), or a combination of the two (as semigloss enamel). These combinations are demonstrated in Figure 5.2.

5.2.   Diffuse reflecting surfaces **(a)** produce no bright images. They appear about equally bright from all viewing angles. Glossy diffusing surfaces **(b)** show a combination of diffuse and specular reflection. The glossy finish produces a bright spot when viewed from the angle of reflection. (*Courtesy of the General Electric Company*)

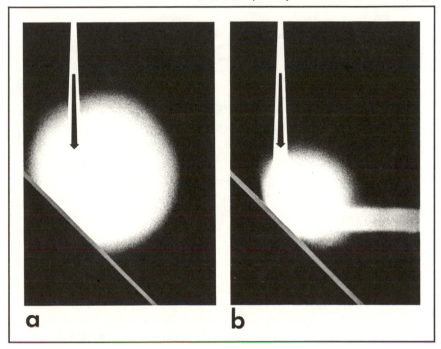

TRANSMISSION

Transmission of light can be either direct (as through clear glass) or diffuse (as through frosted glass). This is shown in Figure 5.3. Diffuse transmission is the principle used in frosted and white bulbs to spread filament image over a larger area, thus producing lower brightness and softer resultant shadows. Diffusers are sometimes used as control devices in fixtures but should be avoided where excessive brightness could be a problem. Chapter 10 discusses some of the application problems with use of diffusers. Where desired, diffusers can be treated for decorative effects.

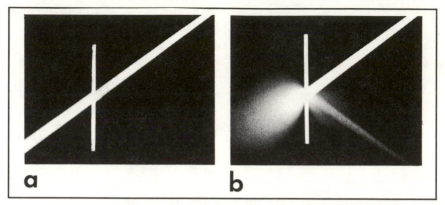

5.3. Direct transmission **(a)** results in almost no change of the light beam, while diffuse transmission **(b)** scatters the light and destroys its directional quality. (*Courtesy of the General Electric Company*)

REFRACTION

Refraction (bending of light rays) is used in lenses to keep brightness out of undesirable viewing angles and place light where wanted. Highly engineered small prisms are formed in plastic or glass and thus can produce light patterns of almost any shape, dependent on source size. Applications of refractive lenses in other than general lighting fixtures are stage spotlights, streetlights, and lighthouses.

ABSORPTION

Absorption is used in fixtures as a method of reducing brightness or changing color. Visible portions of downlights (see Chapter 6) are often painted black to reduce unwanted reflections, while lenses and louvers (vertical baffles) are sometimes tinted to absorb unwanted colors.

POLARIZATION

Polarization of light is a phenomenon that causes the normal random vibrations of light to occur only in a single plane, as indicated in Figure 5.4. The normal view of a light wave coming toward you (if it were visible) would look similar to spokes in a wheel, while after polarization it would appear as a single line. One long-desirable application would be the installation in automobiles of horizontally polarized headlights and vertically polarized windshields. This would allow driving at night with the brights on without causing discomfort to oncoming drivers. This would be difficult to achieve, however, since it would involve changing all headlights and windshields at exactly the same time. Polarization has been applied to light control devices, using the theory that visibility at a given light level is increased because of reduced glare, but the illumination world remains unconvinced.

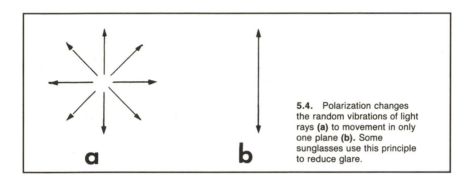

5.4. Polarization changes the random vibrations of light rays **(a)** to movement in only one plane **(b)**. Some sunglasses use this principle to reduce glare.

CONCEALMENT

The principle of concealment is used in structural fixtures such as coves, valances, and cornices (discussed in Chapter 6) and by louvers. They all serve to hide the light source from normal viewing angles, thus producing high visual comfort. Louvers are commonly classified by their shielding angle, meaning the angle above the horizontal at which a lamp becomes visible. A shielding angle of 45 degrees is considered comfortable, while 30 degrees is borderline at best. Formed parabolic louvers not only hide lamp and reflector brightness but also bend the intercepted light downward out of normal viewing angles.

6
FIXTURES

EVERY SPECIFIER HAS BEEN PRESENTED with a "magic" lighting fixture at regular intervals by a visiting salesperson. This fixture is touted as being just right for the current project, no matter what that might be. This chapter will enable the reader to ask intelligent questions regarding the nature of such "magic" gadgets.

FLUORESCENT FIXTURES

A knowledge of basic fluorescent fixture types, because of their wide use, is necessary to anyone even remotely connected with lighting. Sketches in Figure 6.1 clarify the descriptions that follow.

A strip fixture consists of the bare essentials—a wiring channel containing one or more ballasts and associated wires and a pair of lamp holders (or sockets) for each of one, two, or four lamps. They are the cheapest of all fluorescent fixtures and are often used in stores for that reason, even though they provide no means of brightness control.

Industrial fixtures, often called RLM or shop light fixtures, add a reflector to the strip and sometimes a V-shaped divider between lamps to obstruct direct view of the lamp at low crosswise angles. Louvers to decrease end-on brightness are also available.

Wraparounds are a favorite in the commercial trade because they look neat and are inexpensive, but they are often misapplied. They consist of a strip fixture with a plastic shield for appearance and to impart a modicum of light control. While slightly more comfortable than bare lamps, their sides remain far too bright for installation in large offices or classrooms. Use should be limited to spaces where bright fixtures will not cause visual problems.

The workhorse of the commercial fluorescent market is the troffer, whose distinguishing feature is that part or all of it is recessed into the ceiling. It can house one, two, three, or four lamps and usually has a lens or louvers acting as a light-control device on the

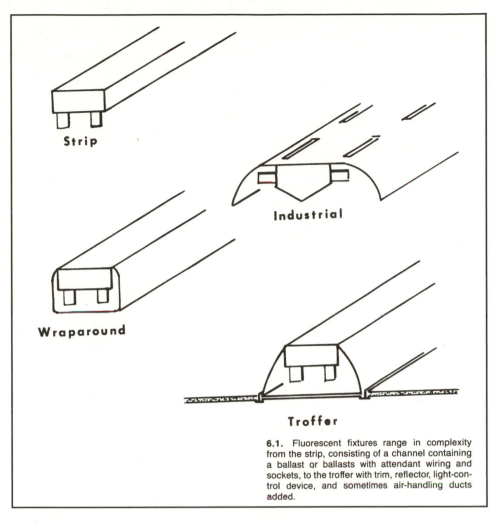

Strip

Industrial

Wraparound

Troffer

6.1. Fluorescent fixtures range in complexity from the strip, consisting of a channel containing a ballast or ballasts with attendant wiring and sockets, to the troffer with trim, reflector, light-control device, and sometimes air-handling ducts added.

bottom. Most popular is the 2- by 4-foot variety, although other dimensions are available, such as 1 by 4 feet, 2 by 2 feet (Figure 6.2), 2 by 5 feet, and so on.

6.2. A 2- by 2-foot troffer operating three 40-watt **U**-shaped lamps. (*Courtesy of the General Electric Company*)

Surface-mounted fixtures come in a variety of forms, with solid, lensed, or diffusing side panels. They are distinguished by the fact that they are mounted flush to the ceiling rather than hung on stems or recessed. Most residential fluorescent fixtures are designed for surface mounting.

Indirect fixtures, sometimes built into office furniture, have come back in vogue to supply the ambient, or walking around, part of the lighting plan known as task/ambient. (See Chapter 13 for discussion.) They are available in a variety of shapes and colors, can hang by stems from the ceiling, and contain one or more lamps.

INCANDESCENT FIXTURES

The only ingredients absolutely necessary for an incandescent fixture are a socket and wires to supply power. Other parts (shades, reflectors, baffles) are extras. A recent trend toward period effects by use of bare bulbs in work areas has led to other memories of yester-year — eyeshades and raging headaches.

Most incandescent fixtures have a marking in them stating "Use no higher than 60-watt bulbs" or some such warning. The size indicated is determined by extensive testing to ensure that no part of the fixture will become a fire hazard in normal use. Do not overload the fixture.

Portable lamps, both floor and table models, provide the bulk of light for most homes. Visual discomfort may arise from their use because they are usually thought of as a decorating rather than a lighting tool. Engineering design often results in too little light on the seeing task and/or too much brightness toward the eye. The most comfortable portable lamps on the market are the ones equipped with diffusers under or over the bulb. Unfortunately, these are not always the most attractive.

Improperly designed shades, as in Figure 6.3, are the main cause of uncomfortable residential portable lamps. The perfect shade at the perfect height will spread light from the bulb over its entire surface, obstruct direct view of the bulb when occupants are either seated or standing, and have approximately the same brightness inside and outside. Perfect height for the bottom of the shade is about 40 inches above the floor, assuming normal seating. (Some problems are illustrated in Figure 12.8.)

Pull-down fixtures are sometimes installed in breakfast nooks or dining rooms and are quite versatile, but they often have an

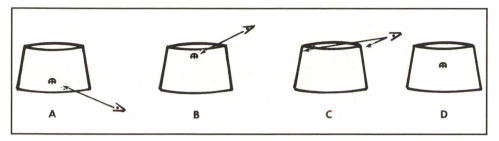

6.3. Improperly designed lamp shades cause most home lighting problems. Incorrect size or position can result in exposure to bulb brightness **(A, B)**, too dense a shade can bring about high contrast between inside and outside **(C)**, while one too sheer allows bulb brightness to show through **(D)**.

opaque top that can create a cavelike effect unless some other light source is used to brighten the ceiling. The same principle applies to some of the modernistic floor lamps.

Chandeliers come in almost limitless forms, prices, and arms and are used to enrich the room appearance. When they are also used to provide working light, as over a dining room table that often doubles for other purposes, most emit insufficient light. If lamp wattage is increased to supply more light, they become far too bright. Ideally, chandeliers should be lamped just high enough in wattage so they are not too bright and then should be dimmed for varying activities.

Downlights, sometimes called "cans," can be fully recessed into the ceiling (see Figures 12.1, 12.2), semirecessed with part of the fixture sticking out into the room, or surface mounted. They can be as simple as a cylinder with a socket in one end and open at the other, or they can be quite complicated. The simple ones, without an internal reflector, should be lamped with PAR or R lamps (see Chapter 4), but in practice general-service bulbs are often used because of the lower price. More than half the generated light is absorbed by these fixtures when the proper lamp is not used.

Downlights having an internal reflector are more expensive than the simple ones and are designed for use with inexpensive general-service lamps. Reflector design determines whether the light beam will be narrow; wide, as shown in Figure 12.2; or asymmetric. The latter is used to light or "wash" walls to a uniform brightness. One variety of downlight called "multiplier" is designed for PAR or R lamps and has a reflector to redirect wide-angle light downward.

Track lights are widely used (sometimes excessively) (Figure 12.4) and range all the way from simple sockets using bare bulbs to highly sophisticated framing spots with user-variable beam spreads. Fixture shapes, colors, and sizes seem to change with each issue of manufacturers' catalogs and all can be mounted on that particular brand of track, a device that mechanically holds and electrically feeds the fixtures. Switches and dimmers for individual fixtures can be added, providing the utmost in versatility. Misuse of track occurs when the fixtures visually intrude on the space. Less obtrusive systems can often be used to accomplish the same lighting goal.

Other incandescent fixture types are indirect wall sconces for general illumination, pole lights (often called "contemporary" but with a lighting effect some would call "deplorable"), ceiling-mounted general lighting fixtures, and high-intensity lamps that are useful for adding light in small areas but quite uncomfortable when used without other sources. Lights sold for specialized purposes, such as picture or piano lights, are often poorly designed and usually give unsatisfactory results.

STRUCTURAL SYSTEMS

The goals of every lighting design should be to provide enough of the right kind of light to perform all seeing tasks easily, enhance design features, and still keep the occupants unaware of the light source. The latter goal is accomplished by minimum brightness differences between the source and its surroundings. The structural lighting fixtures described in this section are often best equipped to attain all these ends.

Figure 6.4 shows that light can be cast in any general direction by judicious choice of lighted structural elements. Use of any of these lighting tools results in soft, even illumination; sparkle and shadowing must be added by other methods. The inside of all structural elements should be painted flat white for maximum efficiency. Fluorescent strips (discussed earlier) are normally used as the light source, although neon tubing (more expensive) can be used if sharply curved forms are required.

A lighted cornice consists of a vertical element (normally just a board) mounted on the ceiling with a fluorescent strip behind it. All the light comes down along the wall or draperies, while the source remains hidden.

A valance differs from a cornice by having space between it and the ceiling to allow light to wash across the ceiling. Cornices and valances on window walls should be just long enough to cover the draperies. A very effective outside finish for both elements is the

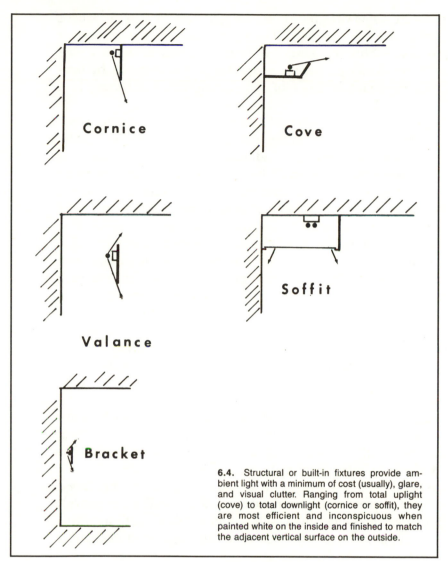

Cornice

Cove

Valance

Soffit

Bracket

6.4. Structural or built-in fixtures provide ambient light with a minimum of cost (usually), glare, and visual clutter. Ranging from total uplight (cove) to total downlight (cornice or soffit), they are most efficient and inconspicuous when painted white on the inside and finished to match the adjacent vertical surface on the outside.

drapery material over padding (see Figure 12.7). If electrical codes permit, power can be drawn from a nearby convenience outlet with the cord and an in-line switch hidden behind the drapery.

A valance (light up and down) becomes a bracket when it is moved down to standing eye level. Predominant uses for brackets are in private offices over couches or under pictures, framed degrees, etc., and in optical examining rooms. Commercially available brackets and valances come in a variety of finishes and shapes.

Coves are somewhat the reverse of cornices in that they have light coming out the top only. The light thus directed across the ceiling works well for commercial or residential spaces that are high enough. A particularly attractive cove for a corridor can be constructed of pegboard in front of fluorescent strips, resulting in a sparkly, starry effect.

Soffits differ from cornices by being wider and having some form of light-control device in the bottom. They commonly appear over kitchen sinks with either incandescent and fluorescent lamps as sources. A variation on the soffit has an open top and is dropped from the ceiling so that light spills out over the ceiling as from a cove. Mounted over a bathroom sink as in Figure 12.11, it provides light both for seeing tasks at the mirror and for general lighting.

A soffit extending from wall to wall becomes a luminous ceiling and in large spaces exudes the same feeling as an overcast day. Possibly for that reason luminous ceilings are in decreasing use even though they remain a versatile, efficient, and inexpensive way to light a space. All that is needed is wall-to-wall light-control material (lens, diffuser, or louver) and fluorescent strips mounted on the structural ceiling. If more light is needed, you just add more strips. All the ugly pipes, ducts, sprinkler heads, etc., are hidden above the light-control media. Ceiling brightness limits acceptable light levels to about 70 footcandles.

In summary, cornices are handy for draperies, murals, and low ceilings where other forms of luminous elements cannot be used; valances work well over windows; brackets are best at eye level to lighten walls in private offices and over couches and under portraits, diplomas, and the like. Coves, with all the light going up, produce a soft feeling and are great for high ceilings, while soffits can provide work light over dressing tables, sinks, and similar locations. More uses for structural elements are discussed and illustrated in Chapter 12.

HIGH-INTENSITY DISCHARGE FIXTURES

Direct and indirect fixtures for high-intensity discharge (HID) lamps have been used with mixed results for general lighting in offices and stores. They can be floor, wall, or ceiling mounted (Figure 6.5) and usually contain a 250- or 400-watt metal halide or high-pressure sodium lamp. The floor standing units (occupying expensive floor space) have tops above normal eye height and are available

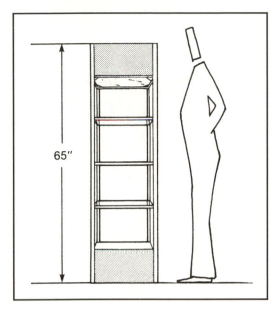

6.5. Indirect high-intensity discharge fixtures can be freestanding as shown or mounted from the wall, ceiling, or work station. (*Courtesy of the McGraw-Edison Company*)

with shelving for displays or plants. Some of the wall or partition-mounted units have openings in the bottom to provide direct illumination to nearby work stations. Distracting ceiling brightness patterns can result from poor reflector design, too low a ceiling, or an insufficient number of fixtures.

7

LIGHTING CONTROLS

LIGHTING CONTROLS VARY ALL THE WAY from simple wall switches to computer-controlled ones that can respond to body heat, movement, outside light, and other increasingly complex influences. The aim of such controls, of course, is to dim or turn the lights on and off in response to need.

Circuit breakers or contactors are used with large electrical loads. They allow manual control of all the lights on a floor, a portion thereof, or in an entire building. The advantage of such centralized control is that occupants cannot leave lights on when they are not needed. A disadvantage is that a large portion of the system may be energized when not in use.

Switching near the lighted location is the most common control method. Imaginative planning can yield a user mastery over the number of lamps operating in each fixture, fixtures per row, whole rows, fractions of rooms, or any combination thereof. The increased cost of such added switches, wire, conduit, and labor during construction is often quickly offset by lower operating costs due to less energy usage.

An increasingly popular switching arrangement is to control one, two, or three lamps in a three-lamp fluorescent fixture and two or four lamps in a four-lamp unit. Three-way switches in homes, giving control at two room entrances, may not be energy-saving devices in themselves, but they do make life a little easier.

Low-voltage control, by which a momentary-contact switch on the wall activates a relay to turn the light on and off, provides an extremely useful design tool. Many lights (or other electrical devices, including outlets, for that matter) can be activated by switch from one position, or one light from many positions. Low-voltage switching is particularly useful in remodeling projects because thin bell wire, usually easier to install, can be used between the switch and fixture instead of more expensive 120-volt wiring. Rotary switches at one location can be used to control all connected lights or outlets. In the home, such switches can be used to turn on all the lights in the house at one time, thus startling any intruders.

Dimmers installed on the wall, in the cord, or on the fixture itself furnish versatility in brightness and light level and are also energy savers. They are normally limited to a total of 600-watts of incandescent lamps (do not use the same ones on fluorescent). Some dimmers cause the filament to produce an audible hum. The only cure to such a problem is to try lamps with different filament shapes, by changing either wattage or voltage, but this is not always successful.

Fluorescent dimming systems with their complicated controls and special ballasts are currently much more expensive than those meant for incandescent fixtures. This situation will be alleviated when electronic ballasts with a built-in dimming circuit are perfected. Many current fluorescent dimming installations, after the initial "look-what-I've-got" period, are used only at off and on levels and perhaps at one other. The same results can usually be obtained much more cheaply with switching.

Timers as lighting controls work well when they are adjusted to the seasons and time changes, but it is common to see the outside lights in used car lots and fast-food restaurants competing with the sun at 10 in the morning or 3 in the afternoon. Often used in the home to control lights at irregular hours to confuse burglars, timers can also be used for turning radios on and off during the owners' absence, regulating plant lights, and starting coffeepots in the morning. Sidereal timers, while more expensive than the standard variety, compensate for shifting daylight hours; some do so for the semiannual time changes.

Photocells depend only on the light level for turning lights on and off, so they are independent of changing seasons and legislative decisions. When it gets dark, they turn the lights on. If a thunderstorm occurs, turning day into night, they turn the lights on and, when it passes, back off. Some are adjustable so that the exact degree of darkness before activation can be regulated. Occasionally, photocells are incorrectly mounted so that the light they control shines on the sensor, making it think dawn has come; the light goes out, then back on, ad infinitum. This situation is normally brought to the owner's attention by attentive neighbors.

The more sophisticated controls that rely on movement, body heat, sound, and the ever-present computer all have the same goal of providing light when and where it is needed. Computers currently turn lights on and off in entire factories and office buildings, while allowing occupant override for late work, unexpected meetings, cleaning, etc. Warehouse aisle lights go on and off in response to movement of lift trucks or people; private offices dim at the departure of the last person, by a cloud obscuring the sun, or by manipulation of a wall control. Office and plant supervisors can turn off or dim unneeded fixtures by punching the proper numbers on a telephone. Street and parking lot lights can be changed from one light level to another at preset times or when traffic or occupancy changes. The future of lighting controls is bright. Technology is already available that allows varying light levels in direct response to need. The next few years will result in reduced costs for these systems and therefore more widespread usage.

8
COSTS

BECAUSE OF RISING ELECTRICITY PRICES, the cost of operating lighting systems has become more important than ever in building design. While scrutiny of lighting costs has traditionally been the province of the electrical engineer, other members of the design team, certainly the owner, are having more and more input. A rudimentary understanding of such costs, both initial and operating, is essential to all designers for self-defense, if for no other reason.

INITIAL COSTS

Initial, or first, costs certainly include lamps and fixtures but also include some items that are not as readily apparent, as shown below:

INITIAL COSTS

Fixtures
Lamps
Wiring cost
   Labor
   Material
Installation labor

The cost of moving power from the point in the building (often called "entrance") where the electrical contractor takes over to and including the box feeding the fixture is called "wiring cost" in lighting cost analyses. This term includes both labor and wire, connectors, conduit or "pipe," contactors, switches, dimmers (if used), circuit breakers, and all the other devices used to turn the lights on and off. The current rule of thumb is that it costs about $200 to connect 1 kilowatt (1000 watts) of lighting load. If 4000 watts (4 kilowatts) of power is needed to light a space, it will therefore cost about $800 for material and labor to move power to the fixtures. Like any rule of thumb this one is seldom exact, but lacking better numbers, it is surprisingly accurate.

The fixtures must be unpacked and sometimes assembled and lamped, although often the latter two steps are taken at the factory. Then they are mechanically and electrically connected. All these costs are usually referred to as "installation labor."

OPERATING COSTS

Operating costs for lighting systems are simpler to enumerate, being only electricity, labor to change lamps and clean fixtures, and lamps themselves:

> OPERATING COSTS
> Lamps
> Labor
> Electricity

While lamp cost is often the most visible, with power hidden among other electrical loads, electricity is 80 percent or more of the total cost for fluorescent installations and an even higher portion of incandescent systems.

A simple residential cost decision might be between installation of a 200-watt incandescent fixture or a single-lamp 40-watt fluorescent strip in a laundry room. They both produce about the same amount of light and might do an adequate job for the task involved.

An incandescent fixture suitable for a laundry room would be about $5 and a bulb $1. The $200 per kilowatt rule yields $40 wiring cost ($200 × 200/1000 = $40). Hanging cost, if separated, might be about $5. Total cost of buying the fixture and lamp, supplying power, and installation is $51.

Incandescent fixture	$5.00
Lamp	$1.00
Wiring	$40.00
Installation labor	$5.00
Total initial cost	$51.00

The fluorescent fixture is more costly, perhaps $10, and the tube another $3 or so. Wiring cost for 50 watts (including ballast losses — see Chapter 4) is $10 ($200 × 50/1000 = $10), and installation is more complicated than the incandescent fixture, maybe $10. Total cost is $33. Realistically, the cost of an electrical box in a home is the

same no matter what is connected to it, so the fluorescent installation would actually be about $12 higher than the incandescent.

Fluorescent fixture	$10.00	
Lamp	$ 3.00	
Wiring cost	$10.00	($40.00)
Installation labor	$10.00	
Total initial cost	$33.00	($63.00)

Looking first at the largest operating cost, energy, the incandescent fixture uses 200 watts, the fluorescent, 50, including ballast.
Electrical cost is calculated by watts (power) multiplied by hours, so
if the laundry room lights are operated 1000 hours a year, watts
times hours is 200,000 watt-hours for the incandescent and 50,000
for the fluorescent. Utilities use kilowatt-hours (1000 watt-hours) as
a billing unit, so division by 1000 converts our examples to 200 and
50 kilowatt-hours respectively. Residential electrical rates vary from
less than 5 cents per kilowatt-hour to more than 15 cents, with the
national average currently about 10 cents per kilowatt-hour. Multiplying both 200 and 50 by $.10 shows that the incandescent lamp will
cost $20 to run for a year and the fluorescent only $5. The extra $12
the fluorescent installation cost originally would be paid back in the
first year. This little study does not even take into account the fact
that life of the fluorescent lamp is 20,000 hours, or, in our example,
20 years, while the incandescent lamp at 750 or 1000 hours life
would have to be changed once or more per year. These figures are
summarized in Table 8.1.

The most common method of finding electrical rates in cents

TABLE 8.1.   Comparative costs of incandescent and fluorescent installations

Item	Incandescent	Fluorescent
	Initial Costs	
Ordering code	200A	F40
Fixture cost	$5.00	$10.00
Lamp cost	1.00	3.00
Wiring cost	40.00	10.00[a]
Hanging cost	5.00	10.00
Total initial cost	$51.00	$33.00[b]
	Energy Costs	
Wattage	200	50
Annual cost	$20.00	$5.00

[a]Real-life cost would be $40, the same as incandescent.
[b]$63, using the higher wiring cost ($40–$10).

per kilowatt-hour is to divide the total bill (less arrears), including taxes, demand charges, fuel-adjustment factors, etc., by the total kilowatt-hours used. The latter number might be hard to find on the bill, but it is there someplace, often well camouflaged.

ENERGY-SAVING METHODS IN LIGHTING

Energy-saving methods (read as money-saving) are many and varied and include the following:

1. Use the most efficient lamp, fixture, and ballast (if needed) combination that suits the application for color, wattage, optical control, etc. (see Figure 4.19 for lamp comparison).

2. Provide no more light than required for the seeing task involved. Currently popular light levels are listed in Chapter 10. Use supplementary fixtures for localized difficult tasks.

3. Provide controls enabling users to fit lighting intensities to varying tasks. These may be manual, people sensing, computer operated, or a combination thereof, as discussed in Chapter 7. Simply allow the user to turn the lights off when they are not needed.

4. Utilize daylight whenever possible with due regard for excess brightnesses from uncontrolled windows.

5. Use light-colored room surfaces when they are commensurate with design criteria.

6. Take advantage of the fact that good maintenance practices can reduce the number of fixtures installed and hence energy usage for a given light level.

During all such energy- and money-saving efforts, it should be remembered that the only reason for any lighting system at all is to serve some human activity. Drastic reductions in the amount of light available often wastes that most valuable commodity, human energy.

9

CALCULATIONS

THE CALCULATIONS REQUIRED for successful lighting designs are presented in this chapter with full explanations of the components used therein. The detailed steps outlined should provide nonengineers with the minimum of pain and anguish.

The definition of footcandle, fc = lm/ft², is the basis of all lighting calculations. If all the light generated by the installed lamps could be counted on to reach the *work plane,* normally assumed to be a horizontal surface at desk height (30 inches above the floor), lighting design would be quite simple. We would merely install enough lamps to generate 100,000 lumens, for instance, if we wanted 100 footcandles in a 1000-square-foot space;

$$100 \text{ fc} \times 1000 \text{ ft}^2 = 100,000 \text{ lm}$$

In practice, for the following reasons, only a portion of the lumens emitted by the lamps get to where they can be used:

1. The fixture itself loses light because the reflector, lens, louver, and/or diffuser, and so forth, all absorb some, and more is lost bouncing around among the lamps themselves. Some manufacturers reflect these losses in the term *fixture (luminaire) efficiency* (see Figure 9.5). (See Figure 6.1 for typical fluorescent fixtures.)

2. The room surfaces (walls, floor, and ceiling) do not reflect all the light shining on them. We intuitively think of dark walls absorbing more light than light ones, but the floors and ceilings have an effect also. The machinery or furniture in the space also absorbs light and thus decreases the amount available.

3. Room shape, as illustrated in Figure 9.1, has a great deal of effect on the efficiency of lighting systems. Most of the light emitted by the fixture in Room A will bounce off one or more walls before it gets where it can be used, while much less will be lost in Room B.

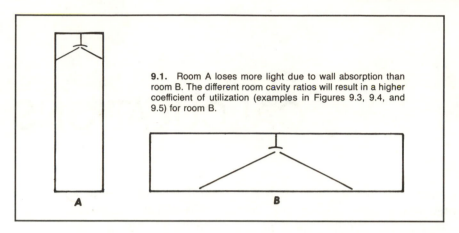

9.1. Room A loses more light due to wall absorption than room B. The different room cavity ratios will result in a higher coefficient of utilization (examples in Figures 9.3, 9.4, and 9.5) for room B.

ROOM RATIO

The terms commonly used in calculations to describe the shape of a space are *room cavity ratio, ceiling cavity ratio,* and *floor cavity ratio.* When used in engineering precision, the floor cavity ratio (FCR) corrects for any difference in reflectance between the walls and floor, while the ceiling cavity ratio performs the same function for the walls and ceiling. Since such corrections are very small except for rooms with a large distance between fixture and ceiling or between floor and work plane, they are commonly disregarded and only the room cavity ratio (RCR) is used. The room cavity ratio defines the relationship of wall area and work plane area. The number actually used is obtained from Table 9.1 or from the following formula:

$$\text{Room cavity ratio} = \frac{5 \times \text{height} \times (\text{length} + \text{width})}{\text{length} \times \text{width}}$$

$$\text{RCR} = \frac{5H \times (L + W)}{L \times W}$$

Note the addition of the seemingly unrelated number (5), which is used primarily to yield an easily handled result. Height (H) in this formula refers to the distance from the fixture to the work plane. Figure 9.2 illustrates two of the various combinations of work plane and fixture height that may be encountered. The importance of the work plane as used in the lumen method of calculating is illustrated by an aircraft repair facility in which the seeing task might be located many feet above the floor.

TABLE 9.1. Determination of cavity ratios

Room Dimensions		Cavity Depth																			
Width	Length	1.0	1.5	2.0	2.5	3.0	3.5	4.0	5.0	6.0	7.0	8	9	10	11	12	14	16	20	25	30
8	8	1.2	1.9	2.5	3.1	3.7	4.4	5.0	6.2	7.5	8.8	10.0	11.2	12.5	—	—	—	—	—	—	—
	10	1.1	1.7	2.2	2.8	3.4	3.9	4.5	5.6	6.7	7.9	9.0	10.1	11.3	12.4	—	—	—	—	—	—
	14	1.0	1.5	2.0	2.5	3.0	3.4	3.9	4.9	5.9	6.9	7.8	8.8	9.7	10.7	11.7	—	—	—	—	—
	20	0.9	1.3	1.7	2.2	2.6	3.1	3.5	4.4	5.2	6.1	7.0	7.9	8.8	9.6	10.5	12.2	—	—	—	—
	30	0.8	1.2	1.6	2.0	2.4	2.8	3.2	4.0	4.7	5.5	6.3	7.1	7.9	8.7	9.5	11.0	—	—	—	—
	40	0.7	1.1	1.5	1.9	2.3	2.6	3.0	3.7	4.5	5.3	5.9	6.5	7.4	8.1	8.8	10.3	11.8	—	—	—
10	10	1.0	1.5	2.0	2.5	3.0	3.5	4.0	5.0	6.0	7.0	8.0	9.0	10.0	11.0	12.0	—	—	—	—	—
	14	0.9	1.3	1.7	2.1	2.6	3.0	3.4	4.3	5.1	6.0	6.9	7.8	8.6	9.5	10.4	12.0	—	—	—	—
	20	0.7	1.1	1.5	1.9	2.3	2.6	3.0	3.7	4.5	5.3	6.0	6.8	7.5	8.3	9.0	10.5	12.0	—	—	—
	30	0.7	1.0	1.3	1.7	2.0	2.3	2.7	3.3	4.0	4.7	5.3	6.0	6.6	7.3	8.0	9.4	10.6	—	—	—
	40	0.6	0.9	1.2	1.6	1.9	2.2	2.5	3.1	3.7	4.4	5.0	5.6	6.2	6.9	7.5	8.7	10.0	12.5	—	—
	60	0.6	0.9	1.2	1.5	1.7	2.0	2.3	2.9	3.5	4.1	4.7	5.3	5.9	6.5	7.1	8.2	9.4	11.7	—	—
12	12	0.8	1.2	1.7	2.1	2.5	2.9	3.3	4.2	5.0	5.8	6.7	7.5	8.4	9.2	10.0	11.7	—	—	—	—
	16	0.7	1.1	1.5	1.8	2.2	2.5	2.9	3.6	4.4	5.1	5.8	6.5	7.2	8.0	8.7	10.2	11.6	—	—	—
	24	0.6	0.9	1.2	1.6	1.9	2.2	2.5	3.1	3.7	4.4	5.0	5.6	6.2	6.9	7.5	8.7	10.0	12.5	—	—
	36	0.6	0.8	1.1	1.4	1.7	1.9	2.2	2.8	3.3	3.9	4.4	5.0	5.5	6.0	6.6	7.8	8.8	11.0	—	—
	50	0.5	0.8	1.0	1.3	1.5	1.8	2.1	2.6	3.1	3.6	4.1	4.6	5.1	5.6	6.2	7.2	8.2	10.2	—	—
	70	0.5	0.7	1.0	1.2	1.5	1.7	2.0	2.4	2.9	3.4	3.9	4.4	4.9	5.4	5.8	6.8	7.8	9.7	12.2	—
14	14	0.7	1.1	1.4	1.8	2.1	2.5	2.9	3.6	4.3	5.0	5.7	6.4	7.1	7.8	8.5	10.0	11.4	—	—	—
	20	0.6	0.9	1.2	1.5	1.8	2.1	2.4	3.0	3.6	4.2	4.9	5.5	6.1	6.7	7.3	8.6	9.8	12.3	—	—
	30	0.5	0.8	1.0	1.3	1.6	1.8	2.1	2.6	3.1	3.7	4.2	4.7	5.2	5.8	6.3	7.3	8.4	10.5	—	—
	42	0.5	0.7	1.0	1.2	1.4	1.7	1.9	2.4	2.9	3.3	3.8	4.3	4.7	5.2	5.7	6.7	7.6	9.5	11.9	—
	60	0.4	0.7	0.9	1.1	1.3	1.5	1.8	2.2	2.6	3.1	3.5	3.9	4.4	4.8	5.2	6.1	7.0	8.8	10.9	—
	90	0.4	0.6	0.8	1.0	1.2	1.4	1.6	2.0	2.5	2.9	3.3	3.7	4.1	4.5	5.0	5.8	6.6	8.3	10.3	12.4
17	17	0.6	0.9	1.2	1.5	1.8	2.1	2.3	2.9	3.5	4.1	4.7	5.3	5.9	6.5	7.0	8.2	9.4	11.7	—	—
	25	0.5	0.7	1.0	1.2	1.5	1.7	2.0	2.5	3.0	3.5	4.0	4.5	5.0	5.5	6.0	7.0	8.0	10.0	12.5	—
	35	0.4	0.7	0.9	1.1	1.3	1.5	1.7	2.2	2.6	3.1	3.5	3.9	4.4	4.8	5.2	6.1	7.0	8.7	10.9	—
	50	0.4	0.6	0.8	1.0	1.2	1.4	1.6	2.0	2.4	2.8	3.1	3.5	3.9	4.3	4.5	5.4	6.2	7.7	9.7	11.6
	80	0.4	0.5	0.7	0.9	1.1	1.2	1.4	1.8	2.1	2.5	2.9	3.3	3.6	4.0	4.3	5.1	5.8	7.2	9.0	10.9
	120	0.3	0.5	0.7	0.8	1.0	1.2	1.3	1.7	2.0	2.3	2.7	3.0	3.4	3.7	4.0	4.7	5.4	6.7	8.4	10.1
20	20	0.5	0.7	1.0	1.2	1.5	1.7	2.0	2.5	3.0	3.5	4.0	4.5	5.0	5.5	6.0	7.0	8.0	10.0	12.5	—
	30	0.4	0.6	0.8	1.0	1.2	1.5	1.7	2.1	2.5	2.9	3.3	3.7	4.1	4.5	4.9	5.8	6.6	8.2	10.3	12.4
	45	0.4	0.5	0.7	0.9	1.1	1.3	1.4	1.8	2.2	2.5	2.9	3.3	3.6	4.0	4.3	5.1	5.8	7.2	9.1	10.9
	60	0.3	0.5	0.7	0.8	1.0	1.2	1.3	1.7	2.0	2.3	2.7	3.0	3.4	3.7	4.0	4.7	5.4	6.7	8.4	10.1
	90	0.3	0.5	0.6	0.8	0.9	1.1	1.2	1.5	1.8	2.1	2.4	2.7	3.0	3.3	3.6	4.2	4.8	6.0	7.5	9.0
	150	0.3	0.4	0.6	0.7	0.8	1.0	1.1	1.4	1.7	2.0	2.3	2.6	2.9	3.2	3.4	4.0	4.6	5.7	7.2	8.6
24	24	0.4	0.6	0.8	1.0	1.2	1.5	1.7	2.1	2.5	2.9	3.3	3.7	4.1	4.5	5.0	5.8	6.7	8.2	10.3	12.4
	32	0.4	0.5	0.7	0.9	1.1	1.3	1.5	1.8	2.2	2.6	2.9	3.3	3.6	4.0	4.3	5.1	5.8	7.2	9.0	11.0
	50	0.3	0.5	0.6	0.8	0.9	1.1	1.2	1.5	1.8	2.2	2.5	2.8	3.1	3.4	3.7	4.4	5.0	6.2	7.8	9.4
	70	0.3	0.4	0.6	0.7	0.8	1.0	1.1	1.4	1.7	2.0	2.2	2.5	2.8	3.0	3.3	3.8	4.4	5.5	6.9	8.2
	100	0.3	0.4	0.5	0.6	0.8	0.9	1.0	1.3	1.6	1.8	2.1	2.4	2.6	2.9	3.1	3.7	4.2	5.2	6.5	7.9
	160	0.2	0.4	0.5	0.6	0.7	0.8	1.0	1.2	1.4	1.7	1.9	2.1	2.4	2.6	2.8	3.3	3.8	4.7	5.9	7.1
30	30	0.3	0.5	0.7	0.8	1.0	1.2	1.3	1.7	2.0	2.3	2.7	3.0	3.3	3.7	4.0	4.7	5.4	6.7	8.4	10.0
	45	0.3	0.4	0.6	0.7	0.8	1.0	1.1	1.4	1.7	1.9	2.2	2.5	2.7	3.0	3.3	3.8	4.4	5.5	6.9	8.2
	60	0.3	0.4	0.5	0.6	0.7	0.9	1.0	1.2	1.5	1.7	2.0	2.2	2.5	2.7	3.0	3.5	4.0	5.0	6.2	7.4
	90	0.2	0.3	0.4	0.6	0.7	0.8	0.9	1.1	1.3	1.6	1.8	2.0	2.2	2.5	2.7	3.1	3.6	4.5	5.6	6.7
	150	0.2	0.3	0.4	0.5	0.6	0.7	0.8	1.0	1.2	1.4	1.6	1.8	2.0	2.2	2.4	2.8	3.2	4.0	5.0	5.9
	200	0.2	0.3	0.4	0.5	0.6	0.7	0.8	1.0	1.1	1.3	1.5	1.7	1.9	2.0	2.2	2.6	3.0	3.7	4.7	5.6
36	36	0.3	0.4	0.6	0.7	0.8	1.0	1.1	1.4	1.7	1.9	2.2	2.5	2.8	3.0	3.3	3.9	4.4	5.5	6.9	8.3
	50	0.2	0.4	0.5	0.6	0.7	0.8	1.0	1.2	1.4	1.7	1.9	2.1	2.5	2.6	2.9	3.3	3.8	4.8	5.9	7.2
	75	0.2	0.3	0.4	0.5	0.6	0.7	0.8	1.0	1.2	1.4	1.6	1.8	2.0	2.3	2.5	2.9	3.3	4.1	5.1	6.1
	100	0.2	0.3	0.4	0.5	0.6	0.7	0.8	0.9	1.1	1.3	1.5	1.7	1.9	2.1	2.3	2.6	3.0	3.8	4.7	5.7
	150	0.2	0.3	0.3	0.4	0.5	0.6	0.7	0.9	1.0	1.2	1.4	1.6	1.7	1.9	2.1	2.4	2.8	3.5	4.3	5.2
	200	0.2	0.2	0.3	0.4	0.5	0.6	0.7	0.8	1.0	1.1	1.3	1.5	1.6	1.8	2.0	2.3	2.6	3.3	4.1	4.9
42	42	0.2	0.4	0.5	0.6	0.7	0.8	1.0	1.2	1.4	1.6	1.9	2.1	2.4	2.6	2.8	3.3	3.8	4.7	5.9	7.1
	60	0.2	0.3	0.4	0.5	0.6	0.7	0.8	1.0	1.2	1.4	1.6	1.8	2.0	2.2	2.4	2.8	3.2	4.0	5.0	6.0
	90	0.2	0.3	0.3	0.4	0.5	0.6	0.7	0.9	1.0	1.2	1.4	1.6	1.7	1.9	2.1	2.4	2.8	3.5	4.4	5.2
	140	0.2	0.2	0.3	0.4	0.5	0.5	0.6	0.8	0.9	1.1	1.2	1.4	1.5	1.7	1.9	2.2	2.5	3.1	3.9	4.6
	200	0.1	0.2	0.3	0.4	0.4	0.5	0.6	0.7	0.9	1.0	1.1	1.3	1.4	1.6	1.7	2.0	2.3	2.9	3.6	4.3
	300	0.1	0.2	0.3	0.3	0.4	0.5	0.5	0.7	0.8	0.9	1.1	1.3	1.4	1.5	1.7	1.9	2.2	2.8	3.5	4.2
50	50	0.2	0.3	0.4	0.5	0.6	0.7	0.8	1.0	1.2	1.4	1.6	1.8	2.0	2.2	2.4	2.8	3.2	4.0	5.0	6.0
	70	0.2	0.3	0.3	0.4	0.5	0.6	0.7	0.9	1.0	1.2	1.4	1.5	1.7	1.9	2.0	2.4	2.7	3.4	4.3	5.1
	100	0.1	0.2	0.3	0.4	0.4	0.5	0.6	0.7	0.9	1.0	1.2	1.3	1.5	1.6	1.8	2.1	2.4	3.0	3.7	4.5
	150	0.1	0.2	0.3	0.3	0.4	0.5	0.5	0.7	0.8	0.9	1.1	1.2	1.3	1.5	1.6	1.9	2.1	2.7	3.3	4.0
	300	0.1	0.2	0.2	0.3	0.3	0.4	0.5	0.6	0.7	0.8	0.9	1.0	1.1	1.3	1.4	1.6	1.9	2.3	2.9	3.5
60	60	0.2	0.2	0.3	0.4	0.5	0.6	0.7	0.8	1.0	1.2	1.3	1.5	1.7	1.8	2.0	2.3	2.7	3.3	4.2	5.0
	100	0.1	0.2	0.3	0.3	0.4	0.5	0.5	0.7	0.8	0.9	1.1	1.2	1.3	1.5	1.6	1.9	2.1	2.7	3.3	4.0
	150	0.1	0.2	0.2	0.3	0.3	0.4	0.5	0.6	0.7	0.8	0.9	1.0	1.2	1.3	1.4	1.6	1.9	2.3	2.9	3.5
	300	0.1	0.1	0.2	0.2	0.3	0.3	0.4	0.5	0.6	0.7	0.8	0.9	1.0	1.1	1.2	1.4	1.6	2.0	2.5	3.0
75	75	0.1	0.2	0.3	0.3	0.4	0.5	0.5	0.7	0.8	0.9	1.1	1.2	1.3	1.5	1.6	1.9	2.1	2.7	3.3	4.0
	120	0.1	0.2	0.2	0.3	0.3	0.4	0.4	0.5	0.6	0.8	0.9	1.0	1.1	1.2	1.3	1.5	1.7	2.2	2.7	3.3
	200	0.1	0.1	0.2	0.2	0.3	0.3	0.4	0.5	0.5	0.6	0.7	0.8	0.9	1.0	1.1	1.3	1.5	1.8	2.3	2.7
	300	0.1	0.1	0.2	0.2	0.2	0.3	0.3	0.4	0.5	0.6	0.7	0.7	0.8	0.9	1.0	1.2	1.3	1.7	2.1	2.5
100	100	0.1	0.1	0.2	0.2	0.3	0.3	0.4	0.5	0.6	0.7	0.8	0.9	1.0	1.1	1.2	1.4	1.6	2.0	2.5	3.0
	200	0.1	0.1	0.1	0.2	0.2	0.3	0.3	0.4	0.4	0.5	0.6	0.7	0.7	0.8	0.9	1.0	1.2	1.5	1.9	2.2
	300	0.1	0.1	0.1	0.2	0.2	0.2	0.3	0.3	0.4	0.5	0.5	0.6	0.7	0.7	0.8	0.9	1.1	1.3	1.7	2.0
150	150	0.1	0.1	0.1	0.2	0.2	0.2	0.3	0.3	0.4	0.5	0.5	0.6	0.7	0.7	0.8	0.9	1.1	1.3	1.7	2.0
	300	—	0.1	0.1	0.1	0.1	0.2	0.2	0.2	0.3	0.3	0.4	0.5	0.5	0.6	0.6	0.7	0.8	1.0	1.2	1.5
200	200	—	0.1	0.1	0.1	0.1	0.2	0.2	0.2	0.3	0.3	0.4	0.5	0.5	0.6	0.6	0.7	0.8	1.0	1.2	1.5
	300	—	0.1	0.1	0.1	0.1	0.1	0.2	0.2	0.2	0.3	0.3	0.4	0.4	0.5	0.5	0.6	0.7	0.8	1.0	1.2
300	300	—	—	0.1	0.1	0.1	0.1	0.1	0.2	0.2	0.2	0.3	0.3	0.3	0.4	0.4	0.5	0.5	0.6	0.7	0.8
500	500	—	—	—	—	0.1	0.1	0.1	0.1	0.1	0.1	0.2	0.2	0.2	0.2	0.2	0.3	0.3	0.4	0.5	0.6

Source: Courtesy of the Illuminating Engineering Society of North America.
Note: When used for room cavity ratio, cavity depth means the distance from the work plane to the bottom of the fixture.

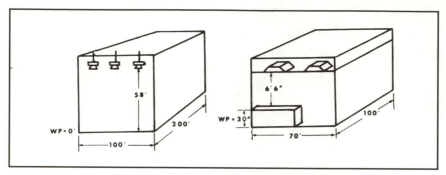

9.2. The distance from work plane to fixture bottom in determining room cavity ratio can vary greatly in different installations. (*Courtesy of the General Electric Company*)

EXAMPLE 1. A 22- by 30-foot room with a 9-foot ceiling is planned, using recessed fixtures and a normal 2.5-foot work plane; height in this case would be 6.5 feet, that is, 9-foot mounting height less the 2.5-foot work plane:

9 ft MH − 2.5 ft WP = 6.5 ft H

The formula then becomes:

$$RCR = \frac{5 \times 6.5 \times (30 + 22)}{30 \times 22} = 2.56 \quad (2.6)$$

Use of Table 9.1 also yields about 2.6, as indicated in Table 9.2.

TABLE 9.2. **Interpolation of Table 9.1 when applied to Example 1**

		Cavity depth		
Width	Length	6.0	(6.5)	7.0
20	20	3.0		3.5
	30	2.5	(2.7)	2.9
	45	2.2		2.5
(22)			(2.6)	
24	24	2.5	(2.7)	2.9
	(30)		(2.5)	
	32	2.2	(2.4)	2.6

EXAMPLE 2. A 50- by 100-foot building with a 25-foot ceiling is being used as a sail loft in which much of the work is done on the floor (zero-foot work plane). If fixtures are hung on 18-inch stems, the system would have a 23.5-foot height. The room cavity ratio would be calculated as follows:

$$RCR = \frac{5 \times 23.5 \times (100 + 50)}{100 \times 50} = 3.525 \quad (3.5)$$

Interpolation in Table 9.1 also yields about 3.5, as shown in Table 9.3.

TABLE 9.3. Interpolation of Table 9.1 when applied to Example 2

Width	Length	Cavity depth 20	(23.5)	25
50				
	70	3.4		4.3
	100	3.0	(3.5)	3.7

Since many other roundings, plus guesses and errors, will be encountered in further calculations, there is no need for such accuracy as 2.56 or 3.525 and these room cavity ratios should be rounded to one decimal point as 2.6 and 3.5.

COEFFICIENT OF UTILIZATION

Manufacturers measure the brightness of their fixtures from all directions at various angles and publish the results as *candlepower curves* in catalog sheets. Typical catalog pages are shown in Figures 9.3 through 9.5. Curves from different fixtures can be compared to choose the one most closely matching the light pattern desired. A fixture with wide distribution, as shown in Figure 9.4, might be fine for a machine shop requiring light under parts of the mechanisms but would be inappropriate for an office devoted to video display tubes. Fixture brightness would be reflected into the operator's eyes, obscuring information on the tube. (See Chapter 13 for a more detailed discussion of this growing problem.)

The candlepower curves are used to calculate fixture efficiency and to compute *coefficient of utilization* tables, examples of which are shown in Figures 9.3 through 9.5. The coefficient of utilization indicates the combined effect of fixture efficiency, room shape (RCR), and surface reflectances on the light emitted by the lamps. The simplest explanation of this term is as the percentage of light leaving the light bulbs that eventually makes its way down to where it can be used.

Catalog sheets typically contain candlepower curves taken in one or more planes, a coefficient of utilization table, and another piece of valuable information called *spacing to mounting height ratio* (S/MH) or *spacing criterion* (SC). This latter information merely indicates how far apart fixtures may be mounted in relation to their

9.3. Portions of catalog sheets for 2- by 2-foot troffer and a wrap-around intended for corridor use. See Chapter 6 for descriptions and sketches of troffers and wraparounds. (*Courtesy of Lighting Products, Inc.*)

Photometric Data

Coefficients of Utilization

Holophane Research and Development Center Test No. 29192. Based on two 2950-lumen lamps, using zonal cavity method.

Floors				20%					
Ceilings	80%			70%			50%		
Walls	70%	50%	30%	70%	50%	30%	50%	30%	10%
1	.69	.66	.64	.67	.65	.63	.62	.61	.59
2	.64	.59	.56	.62	.58	.55	.56	.54	.51
3	.59	.53	.49	.58	.53	.49	.51	.47	.45
4	.55	.48	.43	.53	.47	.43	.46	.42	.39
5	.50	.43	.38	.49	.43	.38	.41	.37	.34
6	.47	.39	.34	.46	.39	.34	.38	.33	.30
7	.43	.35	.30	.42	.35	.30	.34	.30	.27
8	.40	.32	.27	.39	.31	.27	.31	.26	.23
9	.37	.29	.24	.36	.28	.24	.28	.23	.20
10	.34	.26	.21	.33	.26	.21	.25	.21	.18

Candlepower Distribution

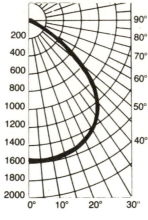

Average Luminance in Footlamberts

Vertical Angles	Average Brightness	
	Across Axis	Along Axis
45°	1383	1103
55°	819	736
65°	676	624
75°	696	666
85°	487	517

Luminaire Efficiency	Spacing Not To Exceed 1.35 x Mtg. Hght.	Maintenance Factors	
62%		Good	.75
		Medium	.70
		Poor	.65

Construction Details

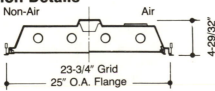

Non-Air   Air

4-29/32"

23-3/4" Grid
25" O.A. Flange

DISTRIBUTION

17.5%

82.5%

Luminaire
Efficiency
74.0%

LUMINAIRE BRIGHTNESS

	Luminaire Brightness in Footlamberts	
	Average Brightness	
Angle	Cross-wise	Length-wise
45°	1512	1087
55°	854	558
65°	444	401
75°	362	381
85°	330	462

CANDLEPOWER DISTRIBUTION

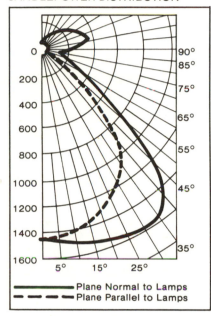

— Plane Normal to Lamps
-- Plane Parallel to Lamps

SPACING

For Maximum
Uniformity,
Spacing Not
To Exceed
1.6 x Mtg. Hght.
(Work Plane
To Ceiling)

MAINTENANCE FACTOR

Good	.75
Medium	.70
Poor	.65

COEFFICIENTS OF UTILIZATION

Zonal Cavity Method

Data is for 2-lamp unit, utilizing 3250 lumen lamps. Independent Testing Laboratories, Inc. report 14392C

FLOORS	20%					
CEILING	80%			50%		
WALLS	50%	30%	10%	50%	30%	10%
1	.75	.72	.70	.67	.65	.63
2	.67	.62	.59	.60	.56	.54
3	.60	.55	.50	.54	.50	.47
4	.54	.48	.44	.48	.44	.41
5	.48	.42	.38	.43	.39	.35
6	.43	.37	.33	.39	.35	.31
7	.39	.33	.29	.36	.31	.27
8	.35	.29	.25	.32	.27	.24
9	.31	.26	.22	.29	.24	.21
10	.28	.23	.19	.26	.21	.18

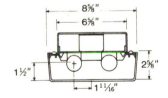

67

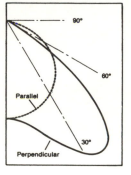
9.4. Part of a catalog sheet for a parabolic troffer offering extremely wide spacing criteria. (*Courtesy of Lighting Products, Inc.*)

mounting height (MH) above the work plane without causing dark areas between fixtures. Fixtures (such as those in Figure 9.5, for example) having a lengthwise spacing criterion (SC) of 1.3, could be situated no further apart than about 8.5 feet, measured between fixture centers, when installed in a 9-foot ceiling, assuming the normal 2.5-foot work plane (6.5-foot MH).

$$6.5 \text{ ft MH} \times 1.3 \text{ SC} = 8.45 \text{ ft (maximum spacing)}$$

While the spacing to mounting height ratios for most fluorescent fixtures are on the order of 1.2/1.4, they can be as large as 2.0, as for the fixture discussed in Figure 9.4. Using the same room dimensions as in the previous example, these fixtures could be mounted as far as 13 feet apart on centers:

$$6.5 \text{ ft MH} \times 2.0 \text{ SC} = 13 \text{ ft (maximum spacing)}$$

Figure 9.6 shows the method of determining centerline spacing when used with spacing criteria.

9.6. This diagram shows how centerline spacing is determined for distances between rows and between fixtures in rows.

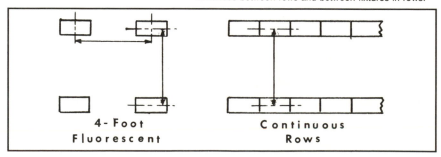

4-Foot Fluorescent

Continuous Rows

Floors									20%										
Ceilings	80%				70%				50%			30%			10%			0%
Walls	70%	50%	30%	10%	70%	50%	30%	10%	50%	30%	10%	50%	30%	10%	50%	30%	10%	0%
1	94	91	88	86	92	89	87	85	86	84	82	82	81	80	80	78	77	76
2	88	83	79	75	86	81	78	74	78	75	73	76	73	71	74	71	70	68
3	82	75	70	66	80	74	70	66	72	68	65	70	66	64	68	65	63	61
4	76	69	63	59	75	68	62	58	66	61	58	64	60	57	62	59	56	55
5	71	62	56	52	69	61	56	52	60	55	51	58	54	51	57	53	50	49
6	66	57	51	46	65	56	50	46	55	50	46	54	49	46	52	48	45	44
7	62	52	46	42	60	51	46	41	50	45	41	49	44	41	48	44	41	39
8	57	47	41	37	56	47	41	37	46	40	37	45	40	36	44	40	36	35
9	53	43	37	33	52	43	37	33	42	36	33	41	36	32	40	36	32	31
10	50	39	33	29	49	39	33	29	38	33	29	38	33	29	37	32	29	28

Candlepower Distribution

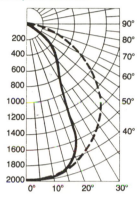

Crosswise ——————
Lengthwise — — — — —

Average Luminance in Footlamberts

Vertical Angles	Average Brightness	
	Lengthwise	Crosswise
0°	1701	1701
45°	1558	608
55°	1413	232
65°	1198	4
75°	806	7
85°	82	20

Luminaire Efficiency:	Luminaire Spacing Criteria:	Maintenance Factors:
83.6%	Lengthwise = 1.3	Good .85%
	45° = 1.1	Medium .80%
	Crosswise = .9	Poor .75%

9.5. Extract from a catalog sheet for one of the many available fixtures designed for specialized applications. Note that it contains an application aid showing suggested usage in addition to the usual crosswise and lengthwise candlepower curves, coefficient of utilization tables, and efficiency, spacing, and maintenance data. (*Courtesy of Lighting Products, Inc.*)

Footcandle levels start decreasing as soon as the system is installed because of two factors — dirt and reduced light output from the lamps. *Lamp lumen depreciation* (LLD) is the term used to describe reduction in light output due to burning time of the lamps. This is evidenced in incandescent lamps by the dark spot above the filament and in fluorescents by a dark ring around the ends. *Luminaire dirt depreciation* (LDD) means the effect of dirt on reflectors, lenses or louvers, lamps, and room surfaces, even though the latter is not indicated in the name. The lamp lumen and luminaire dirt depreciations are sometimes combined into a term called *maintenance factor* (MF) (see Figures 9.3 through 9.5), which is evolved by multiplying the two together:

$$\text{Maintenance factor} = \text{lamp lumen depreciation} \times \text{luminaire dirt depreciation}$$
$$\text{MF} = \text{LLD} \times \text{LDD}$$

The maintenance factor is the most inaccurate of all the values used in estimating light levels because, while lamp manufacturers can accurately forecast lumen depreciation of their products, luminaire dirt depreciation remains at best an educated guess.

Remembering that the definition of a footcandle is one lumen spread over one square foot (fc = lm/ft²) and considering the light-reducing factors of fixture and room efficiencies (contained in the coefficient of utilization) and of the lamp lumen and luminaire dirt depreciations, we can state that the average footcandles maintained in a space will be the total initial lumens delivered by the lamps divided by the area of the room and then reduced by the percentage of light that finally reaches the work plane (CU) and by losses due to dirt and lamp depreciation (MF). In formula form:

$$\text{Footcandles} = \frac{\text{lumens}}{\text{square feet}} \times \text{maintenance factor}$$
$$\times \text{coefficient of utilization}$$
$$\text{fc} = \frac{\text{lm}}{\text{ft}^2} \times \text{MF} \times \text{CU}$$

The term footcandles as used in this formula needs a bit more definition. Properly, it becomes average maintained footcandles. "Average" because the light level thus calculated is not one that would be obtained at every single point in the space but rather an

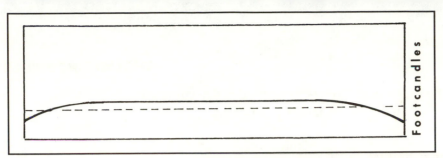

9.7. The dotted line represents average footcandles, while the solid one shows meter readings. Drop-off near walls is due to direct light contribution by fixtures in the center of the room with none from other locations.

average obtained from a regular pattern of readings. Figure 9.7 shows the drop-off near walls. "Maintained" derives from including the debilitating effects of time.

The numbers used in the footcandle formula come from the following sources:

1. Footcandles—from the current range of illumination levels recommended for various seeing tasks by the Illuminating Engineering Society of North America (IESNA) as adjusted for factors of task importance, task brightness, and age of workers.

2. Square feet—from the print or on-site measurement.

3. Maintenance factor and coefficient of utilization—both are usually included in the fixture manufacturer's literature, as in Figures 9.3 through 9.5.

The only item missing in the formula is lumens. Total lumens needed to yield the desired footcandle level is calculated by rearranging the factors above to yield:

$$\text{Lumens} = \frac{\text{footcandles} \times \text{square feet}}{\text{coefficient of utilization} \times \text{maintenance factor}}$$

$$\text{lm} = \frac{\text{fc} \times \text{ft}^2}{\text{CU} \times \text{MF}}$$

The number of lamps required can then be calculated by dividing the total lumens just obtained by the number of lumens generated per lamp. Lumen values can be found in the lamp listing in the Appendix or in manufacturers' catalogs.

$$\text{Number of lamps} = \frac{\text{total lumens}}{\text{lumens per lamp}}$$

$$\text{Lamps} = \frac{\text{Tlm}}{\text{lm/lamp}}$$

The number of fixtures to be used is determined by dividing the number of lamps by the lamps per fixture.

$$\text{Total fixtures} = \frac{\text{lamps}}{\text{lamps per fixture}}$$

$$\text{TF} = \frac{\text{lps}}{\text{lps/F}}$$

This calculation method is also shown in Figure 9.8.

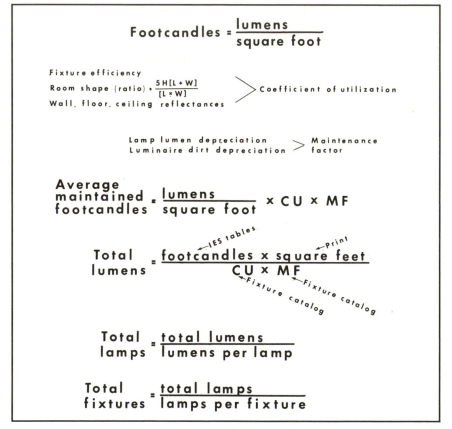

9.8. The derivation, from the basic fc = lm/ft² through the modifying coefficient of utilizaion and maintenance factor, of the full formula for determining average maintained footcandles. Since total lumens is usually the unknown factor, the formula to obtain this number is shown along with sources for the other ingredients.

FIXTURE LAYOUT

Planning the physical placement of fixtures in a space is more of an art than a science, but there are certain steps to follow that can help the uninitiated:

1. Try installing all the fixtures in one row down through the center of the long dimension (Figure 9.9a). If they are fluorescent, you may find that they will not fit without extending into the parking lot, so you will know there is something wrong. (Eight 4-foot fixtures will not work end to end in a 25-foot room.) Also the distance of the row from the parallel wall will almost certainly exceed the maxim illustrated in Figure 9.10 that 4 feet is the maximum distance of fluorescent fixtures from the wall.

9.9. One method of determining fixture placement in a room, showing spacing of **(a)** one row, **(b)** two rows, and **(c)** three rows. Sketch **(d)** shows centerlines of fixtures within rows.

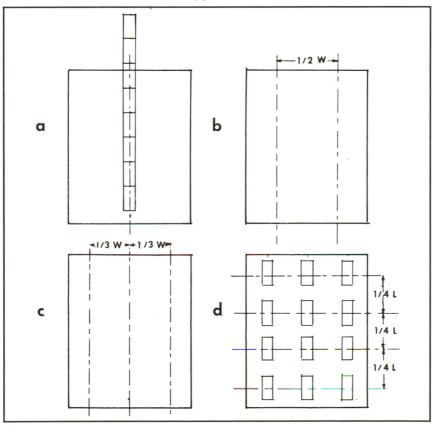

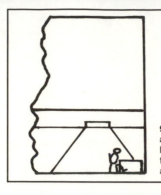

9.10. The overly dark area near the wall caused by mounting fluorescent fixtures further than 4 feet away is indicated here.

2. Try two rows paralleling the long dimension, as in Figure 9.9b. Separate the rows by half the room width (row spacing equals room width divided by two) with one-half the resultant row spacing to each long wall. Check that the spacing to mounting height ratio for the fixture has not been exceeded. If that is all right, be sure the fixtures are not more than 4 feet from the wall.

3. If two rows do not work, try three (Figure 9.9c). Separate the rows by one-third the width of the space (width divided by number of rows) and check the spacing to mounting height ratio and distance to the wall again.

4. Continue this trial-and-error method until an acceptable row-spacing plan is reached. "Spacing" as used here means the distance from centerline to centerline (see Figure 9.6), not from the side of one fixture to the side of the next.

5. Having arrived at a workable number of rows, divide that number into the total fixtures previously calculated to find out how many fixtures are needed in each row. This step rarely results in an even number, so another rounding is usually required to make the rows even.

6. Spacing between fixtures, when continuous rows are not used, is determined in the same manner as that between rows, namely, by dividing row length by number of fixtures to yield the distance between fixture centers along each row, as in Figure 9.9d. Once again rounding comes into play when the resultant number is changed to 1-foot or sometimes 2-foot increments to fit physical requirements of the ceiling.

An alternate spacing method starts with the area to be covered by each fixture. Total area of the room is divided by the number of fixtures required, thus obtaining square feet per fixture. The square root of that number, or the number that when multiplied by itself will yield square feet per fixture, is the theoretical center-to-center spacing desired. Rounding is almost always required to obtain proper spacing increments as determined by ceiling construction and to get manageable distances. This form of layout requires a little practice.

It makes good sense to redo the mathematics before committing a boss's or client's money to a firm lighting design. The check normally used is to go back to the "footcandles =" formula from Figure 9.8, substitute the number of fixtures just obtained, and see what the light level turns out to be. There are also a number of very helpful slide rules and nomographs available from equipment manufacturers.

Neither the engineering method described above nor the pure design way of developing a luminous environment is usually correct when used alone. While the design approach has never been well documented, the classic engineering method can be summarized as follows:

1. Determine the lighting level recommended by IESNA for the seeing tasks to be performed.

2. Decide which light source (fluorescent, high-pressure sodium, or other) is best suited to the required color rendition, efficiency, and control requirements of the installation. As explained in Chapter 4, the highest wattage (most efficient) lamp that meets all the other criteria should be chosen.

3. Determine the fixture type (lensed troffer, indirect, parabolic, or other, as described in Chapter 6) best suited to the task and space.

4. Calculate the number of fixtures required for the desired footcandle level, using the method in Figure 9.8. Note that fractions of fixtures are not available, so that rounding to a whole number is necessary.

5. Design the fixture layout. ("For uniformity" used to be added to this step, but we can no longer afford to light all areas of a space to the same level.)

6. Recalculate the light level to be obtained when using the number of fixtures actually planned.

The steps in this process are summarized as follows:

1. Determine the light level needed.
2. Choose the light source.
3. Choose the fixture type.
4. Calculate the number of fixtures needed.
5. Plan the layout.
6. Recalculate footcandle level.

SAMPLE DESIGN PROBLEM

An office performing general clerical tasks involving typing, filing, etc., measures 24 feet wide by 41 feet long and has a suspended acoustical ceiling 8.5 feet above the floor. Reflectances are determined to be 50 percent for the walls, 50 percent for the ceiling, and 20 percent for the floor.

Using the steps listed above, step 1 is to determine how many footcandles we wish to supply for the seeing task involved. The accepted level for general office work is somewhere between 50 and 100 footcandles, with 80 a current favorite (see Table 10.1). The ultimate source for recommended levels is, of course, the current edition of the *IES Lighting Handbook*.

Step 2 requires choice of a light source. For reasons explained in Chapter 4, that could logically be a 40-watt cool white fluorescent lamp (ordering abbreviation F40CW) with initial light output of 3150 lumens, as shown in Table A.6 in the Appendix.

The fixture chosen in step 3 is often a three-lamp parabolic troffer. (A typical coefficient of utilization table is shown in Figure 9.4.)

Now come the calculations required by step 4. Using the total lumens formula of Figure 9.8, we can readily insert footcandles (80) and square feet (24 × 41 or 984).

$$lm = \frac{80 \times (24 \times 41)}{(CU \times MF)}$$

In the previous discussion of coefficient of utilization it was pointed out that wall, ceiling, and floor reflectances; room shape (RCR); and fixture efficiency all determine the percentage of generated light that finally arrives at the work plane. Note that the coefficient of utilization table in Figure 9.4 is entered by RF (reflectance of the floor cavity) (20 percent), RC (reflectance of the ceiling cavity) (80, 50 percent), and RW (reflectance of the walls) (50, 30, 10 percent). The percentages referred to, of course, are reflectances of the respective surfaces. Remember from earlier discussion that floor and ceiling cavity reflectances can be treated as those of the floor and ceiling without modification for the vast majority of applications. The numbers from 1 to 10 down the left side of the table are room ratios.

Use of the room cavity ratio formula shown earlier yields 1.98, which should be promptly rounded to 2.0.

$$RCR = \frac{5 \times 6 \text{ ft} \times (24 + 41)}{24 \times 41} = 1.98 \quad (2.0)$$

To check this result, use the table of ratios (Table 9.1). Enter with a cavity depth of 6 feet (8.5 − 2.5) and a width of 24 feet. The given length of 41 feet, not shown, is about halfway between the listed values of 32 (CR = 2.2) and 50 (CR = 1.8). Using the interpolation method shown in Table 9.4, the room cavity ratio is also 2.0.

TABLE 9.4. Interpolation of Table 9.1 when applied to the sample design problem

Width	Length	Cavity depth
24		6.0
	32	2.2
	(41)	(2.0)
	50	1.8

Entering the table shown in Figure 9.4 with floor, ceiling, and wall reflectances of 20, 50, and 50 percent respectively and using 2 as a cavity ratio gives a coefficient of utilization equaling 0.79. The maintenance factor suggested for this fixture is 0.85. Including these numbers in the total lumens formula shows the need for 117,230 installed lumens to result in 80 footcandles:

$$lm = \frac{80 \text{ fc} \times 984 \text{ ft}^2}{.79 \text{ CU} \times .85 \text{ MF}} = 117,230$$

The next steps in calculation are to determine the number of lamps and then fixtures required.

$$\text{Lamps} = \frac{117,230 \text{ lm}}{3150 \text{ lm/lamp}} = 37$$

$$\text{Fixtures} = \frac{37 \text{ lamps}}{3 \text{ lamps/fixture}} = 12.33 \quad (12)$$

Since $1/3$ or 0.33 of a fixture is not available, the number 12.33 obtained from the formula is rounded to 12.

Applying the procedure previously outlined for fixture layout, one row of twelve 4-foot fixtures takes up 48 feet, longer than our room, as shown in Figure 9.11a and, when centered parallel to the

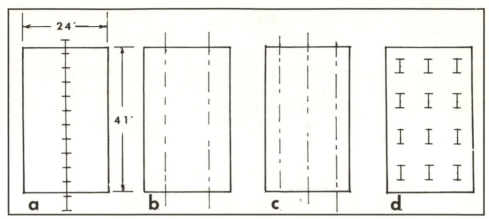

9.11. (a), (b), and (c) illustrate results when one, two, and three rows respectively of 4-foot fixtures are installed in a 24- by 41-foot room; (d) shows fixture spacing within rows for 12 fixtures.

41-foot dimension, is more than the desired 4-foot minimum from the wall. Discard a one-row plan.

Two rows parallel to the long dimension would be symmetrically mounted 12 feet apart (24 feet/2 rows = 12) and 6 feet from the long walls. This is shown in Figure 9.11b. Six feet is too great a distance from the walls, so a two-row plan should be discarded even though a note in Figure 9.4 states, "spacing not to exceed 2.0 × mounting height." Since 2.0 times 8.5 feet equals 17.0, 12-foot spacing would result in even illumination between rows.

Three rows evenly spaced result in an 8-foot distance between rows (well within the manufacturer's spacing to mounting height ratio) and 4 feet from outside rows to the long walls. See Figure 9.11c.

Placement of the fixtures within rows is accomplished in a manner similar to that sketched in Figure 9.11d. Four per row would have fixtures on 10-foot centers with the end of the last fixtures 3.5 feet from the walls.

The next step is to recalculate for light level, using the actual number of fixtures just reached. The calculation would look like this:

$$fc = \frac{12 \text{ fixtures} \times 3 \text{ lamps per fixture} \times 3150 \text{ lm}}{984 \text{ ft}^2}$$

$$\times .79 \text{ CU} \times .85 \text{ MF} = 77$$

This solution would result in a uniform lighting level throughout the space, which may or may not be desirable. Suitable switches, as discussed in Chapter 7, should be installed to allow occupants' choice of light levels.

INVERSE SQUARE LAW

The method used to forecast light levels at a point when small sources are used is called the *inverse square law*. In engineerese, the footcandle level resulting from a point source is equal to the brightness of that source in a given direction divided by the square of its distance from that source. In formula form:

$$\text{Footcandles} = \text{candlepower/distance squared}$$
$$fc = cp/D^2$$

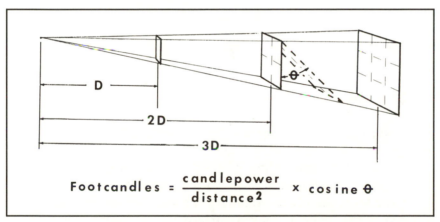

$$\text{Footcandles} = \frac{\text{candlepower}}{\text{distance}^2} \times \text{cosine } \theta$$

9.12. The area covered by a given bundle of light increases by the square of the distance from a point source and also at incident angles other than 90 degrees, thus decreasing resultant footcandles. These facts give rise to the inverse square law.

As indicated in Figure 9.12, the resultant number must be multiplied by the cosine of the incident angle subtracted from 90 degrees. (No adjustment is needed for 90 degrees because the cosine of 0 degrees is 1.0.) Cosine values for other angles are given in Table 9.5. The point-by-point method normally neglects the maintenance factor, resulting, of course, in initial footcandles only.

An example of the rule would be a 1000-candlepower spotlight shining directly on a wall 10 feet away. A light meter aimed at the

TABLE 9.5.   Cosine values of common angles for use with the inverse square law

Degree	Value	Degree	Value
0°	1.0	45°	0.707
5°	0.996	50°	0.643
10°	0.985	55°	0.574
15°	0.966	60°	0.5
20°	0.940	65°	0.423
25°	0.906	70°	0.342
30°	0.866	75°	0.259
35°	0.819	80°	0.174
40°	0.766	85°	0.087

light from the wall would read 10 footcandles:

$$1000/(10 \times 10) = 10$$

When the light is moved to a 5-foot distance, the reading will be quadrupled to 40 footcandles:

$$1000/(5 \times 5) = 40$$

If the distance were doubled, the reading would drop to one-fourth of the original, or 2.5 footcandles:

$$1000/(20 \times 20) = 2.5$$

Major applications of the inverse square law are for washing walls with light and for spotlighting. Manufacturers of fixtures used for these purposes do the calculating required and display the results in their catalogs. An example of such an aid for wall-washing is shown in Figure 9.13. Simply by following the step-by-step instructions, a designer can light a vertical surface to the desired level without unsightly dark or bright areas.

Referring to Figure 9.13, the ratio S/D is critical to a satisfactory lighting job. If S (spacing distance between fixtures) is too wide or D (distance from fixture to wall) is too small, dark areas will result.

Each manufacturer has slightly different guides for use of its fixtures, but a good rule of thumb to follow, lacking better information, is to mount wall-washing fixtures no nearer the wall than one-fourth the height of the wall. On an 8-foot wall, for example, fixtures should be at least 2 feet away. A greater distance will result in more even illumination.

Another use of the inverse square law is to determine the source brightness needed to provide a desired light level. In formula form:

$$\text{Candlepower} = \text{footcandles} \times \text{distance squared}$$
$$\text{cp} = \text{fc} \times D^2$$

RULES OF THUMB

This section will deal with three of the myriad rules of thumb that abound in the lighting industry. Many are just plain wrong, all have limitations and all should be used with care.

HALF THE LIGHT GETS TO THE WORK PLANE. This maxim states that over the life of the system, half the light installed never gets down to where it can be used, so by merely doubling the result of multiplying footcandles by square feet (remember, fc = lm/ft^2), the number of total initial lumens to be installed can be obtained.

This rule is logical, since in large office spaces with good reflectances a fairly efficient fluorescent fixture has a coefficient of utilization of about 0.70 (70 percent), and a maintenance factor of about 0.70 (70 percent). When 0.70 is multiplied by 0.70, the resultant 0.49 is close enough to 0.50 to be called half. To use this rule, just multiply the number of total maintained footcandles needed by the area and double that number to find the required total initial lumens. Easy—right?

The limitations involved are:

1. Efficient lamps (cool white, warm white, light white, and others).
2. Efficient fixtures (bare lamps, wraparounds, lensed troffers, large-cell parabolics).
3. Medium or large offices (width at least twice height).
4. Light room surfaces (at least 50 percent reflectance of walls and ceilings).

Deviation from any one of these limitations negates the rule.

An example would be an office of 1000 square feet (about 33 feet long by 33 feet wide) being designed for 100 footcandles. The 100 footcandles (lm/ft^2) times 1000 square feet yields 100,000 lumens required at the work plane. Twice that is 200,000, which is what should be installed.

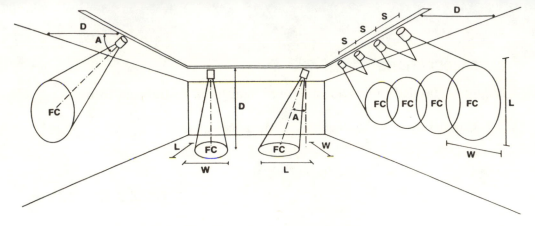

Track application illustration, letter code key

A Aiming angle

D Distance to fixture from wall or floor

FC Maximum horizontal footcandles on wall or floor within the effective visual beam

L Effective visual beam length in feet

W Effective visual beam width in feet

EVB Effective Visual Beam, the point that the candle power is reduced to a ratio of 5:1 from the light source

S Spacing, the maximum distance between fixtures for uniform illumination, taking into consideration overlap of beams.

Aiming Angles

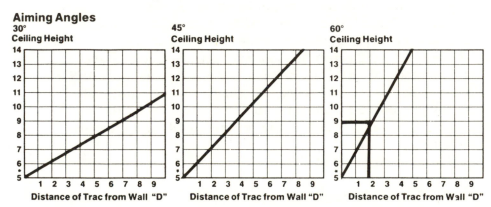

30°
Ceiling Height — Distance of Trac from Wall "D"

45°
Ceiling Height — Distance of Trac from Wall "D"

60°
Ceiling Height — Distance of Trac from Wall "D"

*Average eye level: 65"

Determining Trac Placement and Lamp Selection

Problem: Lighting a Painting. Providing 43 FC's of illumination for a painting centered at standard 65" eye level, on an 9' wall. The artpiece measures 4' high × 5' wide. A 60 degree aiming angle should be used to minimize glare.

Solution:

Consult 60° aiming angle table above. Find the horizontal increment for a wall height of 9'. Follow horizon-tally until you reach the diagonal line which represents the beamspread center. Now go down from this point to find D (distance from wall) for location of trac. For this problem, D = 2'. Next, consult the Lamp Performance Data which begins on page 83. Read 60° aiming angle data until a beam length (L) and width (W), with values of L = 4 and W = 5, with a D value of 2' is found. For this solution, lamp is 75W R30 FL.

Problem: Spacing Lampholders for

Uniform Wall Washing. Establishing necessary spacing of fixtures to maintain 32 FC's of uniform vertical illumination. Trac is mounted 2' from wall with lampholders aimed at 60° angles.

Solution:

Consult the Lamp Performance Data which begins on next page. Read 60° aiming angle to locate 32 FC's with a D (Distance) of 2'. Read across to S (Spacing) column. Result is 50W R20 FL spaced 3 feet apart.

9.13. A typical application aid, showing the method for choosing light sources, fixture spacing, and mounting distance for a wall-washing problem. (*Courtesy of the McGraw-Edison Company*)

Lamp	Beam Spread	0° Aiming Angle					30° Aiming Angle					45° Aiming Angle					60° Aiming Angle				
		D	FC	L	W	S	D	FC	L	W	S	D	FC	L	W	S	D	FC	L	W	S
75W R30 SP Rated Life 2,000	41.1° x 41.1°	4	102	3	3	3	3	118	3	2	2	3	70	5	3	3	2	69	5	2	2
		6	45	4	4	4	5	42	5	4	4	4	39	6	4	4	3	31	7	4	3
		8	25	6	6	5	7	22	7	6	5	5	25	8	5	5	4	17	10	5	4
75W R30 FL Rated Life 2,000	85.2° x 85.2°	3	44	5	5	5	3	36	4	6	5	2	61	3	4	4	1	171	2	2	2
		4	25	7	7	7	4	20	6	8	6	3	27	5	7	6	2	43	4	5	4
		5	16	9	9	9	5	13	7	10	8	4	15	7	9	8	3	19	6	7	6
75W ER 30 Rated Life 2,000	73.7° x 73.7°	4	114	3	3	3	3	132	3	3	3	3	78	4	3	3	2	79	4	3	2
		6	50	6	6	4	5	47	5	5	4	4	44	6	4	4	3	35	7	4	4
		8	28	7	7	6	7	24	7	7	6	5	28	7	5	5	4	20	9	6	5
75W PAR38 SP (cool beam also) Rated Life 2,000	26.3° x 26.3°	6	155	3	3	3	4	215	2	21	2	3	221	2	2	2	2	197	3	3	3
		8	87	4	4	3	6	96	4	3	3	5	80	4	3	3	3	88	5	2	2
		10	56	5	5	4	8	54	5	4	4	7	41	6	4	4	4	47	7	3	3
		12	39	6	6	5	10	34	6	5	5	9	25	7	6	5	5	32	8	4	4
75W PAR38 FL (cool beam also) Rated Life 2,000	41.1° x 41.1°	4	116	3	3	3	3	135	3	2	2	3	83	4	3	3	2	85	5	2	2
		6	52	4	4	4	5	49	5	4	4	4	47	6	4	4	3	38	7	4	4
		8	29	6	6	6	7	25	7	6	6	5	30	7	5	5	4	21	9	5	5
100 W R25 FL (Halo Z10) Rated Life 2,000	66.5° x 66.5°	5	24	6	6	6	5	17	6	7	7	3	33	5	5	5	2	48	4	3	2
		6	17	8	8	7	6	12	8	9	9	4	18	7	7	6	3	21	6	4	4
		8	9	10	10	10	7	9	9	10	10	5	12	8	8	8	4	12	8	6	5
120W ER 40 Rated Life 2,000	44.5° x 44.5°	5	116	4	4	4	4	122	4	4	3	3	130	5	3	3	2	135	4	3	2
		8	45	6	6	5	7	40	7	7	6	5	47	8	6	5	3	60	7	4	4
		11	24	9	9	8	10	20	9	10	8	7	24	11	8	7	4	34	9	6	5
50W PAR36 VNSP 12V Rated Life 2,000	8.5° x 8.2°	10	201	1	1	1	8	203	2	1	1	6	197	2	1	1	4	160	2	1	1
		15	89	2	2	2	12	90	2	2	2	9	88	3	2	2	6	71	3	2	2
		20	50	3	3	3	16	51	3	3	3	12	50	3	3	2	8	40	5	2	2
		25	32	4	4	3	20	33	4	4	3	15	32	4	3	3	10	25	6	3	3
50W PAR36 NSP (Halo Z3) 12V Rated Life 2,000	19.5° x 17.1°	7	188	2	2	2	6	168	3	2	2	4	214	2	2	2	2	336	2	1	1
		10	92	3	3	3	9	75	4	3	3	6	95	4	3	2	3	150	3	2	2
		13	54	4	4	4	12	42	5	4	4	8	54	5	3	3	4	84	5	2	2
		16	36	5	5	5	15	27	7	5	5	10	34	6	4	4	5	54	6	3	3
50W PAR36 WFL 12V Rated Life 2,000	40.0° x 40.8°	3	144	2	2	2	3	104	3	2	2	2	150	2	2	2	1	297	2	1	1
		5	52	4	4	3	5	38	5	4	4	3	67	4	3	3	2	74	3	3	2
		7	26	5	5	5	7	19	6	6	6	4	38	5	4	4	3	33	5	4	3
50W PAR36 VWFL 12V Rated Life 2,000	48.5° x 48.5°	3	67	3	3	3	3	45	3	3	3	2	63	3	2	2	1	121	2	1	1
		4	37	4	4	3	4	25	5	4	4	3	28	4	4	3	2	30	4	3	3
		5	24	4	4	4	5	16	6	5	5	4	16	6	5	5	3	13	6	5	4
50W R20 FL Rated Life 2,000	49.4° x 49.4°	3	60	3	3	3	3	49	3	3	3	2	64	3	3	2	1	23	2	2	1
		4	34	4	4	3	4	27	4	4	4	3	28	5	4	3	2	32	5	3	3
		5	22	5	5	4	5	18	5	5	5	4	16	7	5	5	3	14	7	5	4
Q75 MR16/NSP (Halo Z40) Rated Life 3,500	13° x 12°	16	57	5	5	5	15	44	6	6	5	10	58	6	4	4	5	92	6	3	3
		13	86	4	4	4	12	69	5	5	4	8	91	5	4	3	4	143	5	2	2
		10	146	3	3	3	9	123	4	3	3	6	162	4	3	2	3	255	3	2	2
		7	297	2	2	2	6	276	2	2	2	4	364	2	2	2	2	573	2	1	1
Q75 MR16/FL (Halo Z45) Rated Life 3,500	39° x 39°	10	24	9	9	9	9	22	9	8	8	5	48	7	4	4	4	40	7	4	4
		8	37	7	7	7	7	37	7	6	6	4	75	5	3	3	2	72	5	3	3
		6	66	5	5	5	5	72	5	4	4	3	134	4	3	3	2	161	3	2	2
		4	148	4	4	3	3	199	3	3	3	2	301	3	2	2	1	645	2	1	1

100 fc × 1000 ft² = 100,000 lm (at work plane)
2 × 100,000 lm = 200,000 lm (installed)

With a 40-watt cool white fluorescent tube producing 3150 lumens, about 63.49 (round to 64) lamps are needed, or 16 four-lamp fixtures.

$$\frac{200,000 \text{ lm}}{3150 \text{ lm/lamp}} = 63.49 \text{ lamps (64)}$$

Number rounding as shown above is needed with rules of thumb, as with other lighting calculations, for several reasons. Fixtures come only in whole numbers, not halves or quarters or 0.49s; very seldom do we know exact room reflectances, and the dirt factors used are really no more than educated guesses. After all the figuring is done, the fixtures have to fit into the space with some sort of geometric regularity, and the calculated number is almost always adjusted up or down so that the room will look right. Lighting is not an exact science.

SQUARE FEET PER LAMP OR FIXTURE. In medium or large spaces (with width at least twice ceiling height) having light room surfaces and using high-efficiency, full-wattage lamps and efficient fixtures (ever hear these disclaimers before?), 100 footcandles will result if one 40-watt fluorescent lamp is used for every 12 square feet of space. If less efficient lamps or fixtures are planned, use one lamp for each 10 square feet. If other footcandle levels are planned (say 50, or ½ of 100), a lamp could cover more area, in this case 24 square feet.

The currently popular office light level of 80 footcandles results from installation of one four-lamp lensed troffer for each 64 square feet of space. Fixtures on 8- by 8-foot centers (8 × 8 = 64 ft²) is a widely used system for speculative office buildings (those built for leasing to yet unknown tenants). Note again that none of these rules works for small dark spaces.

WATTS PER SQUARE FOOT. Back when electric utilities were allowed by popular opinion to have sales and/or marketing people, a common rule of thumb among those folks was that 25 footcandles resulted from every watt per square foot of installed fluorescent lamp. You wanted 75 footcandles, you installed 3 watts of fluorescent lamps for every square foot of floor space. Progress in design of lamps, ballasts, and fixtures has rendered this rule *dead wrong!*

SUMMARY

Calculation methods described above certainly do not cover all the variations in applications that may be encountered. The explanations are meant only to provide a basis for further study. Manufacturers often provide excellent aids for use of their fixtures.

10
QUANTITY AND QUALITY

MOST LIGHTING DESIGNS ACCOMPLISH only a portion of the following two goals: (1) provide enough light of the proper quality to perform seeing tasks easily and (2) help achieve the visual goals of the architect and/or designer. The success of a lighting system is usually judged with the aid of a pocket light meter (Figure 10.1) on the basis of footcandles or fixture brightness. Many people erroneously feel that if the fixture looks bright there is enough light.

The common evaluation of installations by footcandle level alone has brought about some legendary deceptive practices. One is the use of either a high- or low-reading light meter to obtain the desired result. Another is judicious use of a white shirt to reflect light onto the meter. Probably the most common and misleading evaluation method is reading light levels in the center of an open space before occupancy and with only a few hours of total use on the lamps. The two problems with this routine are that with symmetrical layouts, levels will always be higher in the center of the space than near walls (see Figure 9.7) and that the debilitating effects of time and dirt have not yet taken place.

Another form of measurement is based on appearance of the space—surface brightnesses. A fallacy of this approach is that the seeing tasks are not usually considered. A dim bar might look great to its nocturnal inhabitants but be impossible to clean up in the morning if working lights are not installed. As discussed in Chapter 14, a shopper, in addition to being visually attracted to a store, needs enough light of the proper quality to appraise the wares. The designer who festoons neon tubing all over a drafting area or lights a computer programmer's work area with unshielded industrial fixtures should be sentenced to a lifetime of filling out income-tax forms under that illumination.

Controversy about adequate light levels has been around since invention of the light bulb, if not before, and flares up anew during

10.1. A low-cost light meter commonly used for evaluation of lighting installations. (*Courtesy of the General Electric Company*)

recessions, depressions, and oil embargoes because of added attention to lighting costs. The Illuminating Engineering Society of North America (IESNA) conducts the only continuing scientific research in this country on quality and quantity of illumination. From time to time, government agencies and industry groups have issued their own footcandle recommendations. Some of these have proved impossible to implement, have had lower values than those of IESNA, and have often been backed only by opinions of the issuing bureaucrats, politicians, or committee members.

Task light levels that are considerably lower than those recommended by the IESNA can cause undesirable effects on productivity as well as wasted human effort, as indicated in Figure 10.2. The wrong quality of light can have the same effects. Official IESNA recommendations are available in its current *Handbook*. Table 10.1

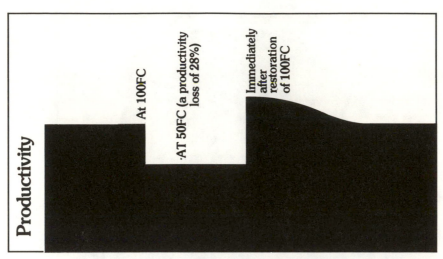

Productivity

At 100FC

AT 50FC (a productivity loss of 28%)

Immediately after restoration of 100FC

10.2. When the illumination level in a social security office was reduced from 100 footcandles to 50 footcandles, the productivity rate fell by 28 percent. With original light levels restored, productivity soared for a short time, then receded to its original level. (*Courtesy of the General Electric Company*)

TABLE 10.1. Current light levels for various seeing tasks

Seeing task	Footcandles
Art galleries	
Ambient	20–30
Featured displays	50+
Assembly	
Rough (lumber)	20–40
Medium (bolts, screws)	40–80
Fine (electronics)	100+
Auditoriums	20+
Banks	
Public areas	30–80
Tellers	60–120
Corridors	10–20
Entrances, active	5
Food preparation	30+
Homes (see specific tasks)	
Loading docks	10–20
Offices, general	80
Parking garages	2–4
Restaurants	
Fast service	40–100
Intimate (liquor served)	0+
Kitchen	50+
Schools, classrooms	70–100
Stairways	10
Stores	
Mass merchandising (few clerks)	60–100
Intimate (many clerks)	20–60
Displays	At least 3 times surrounding brightness
Toilets	15–30
Warehouses	
Inactive	5–20
Active	20+

represents what the author sees currently being used in successful installations, and the light levels quoted therein are based solely on personal opinion.

One effect of low light levels, other than decreased visibility, is that colors lose their intensity. Subtle differences disappear and bright colors die at levels under about 10 footcandles. This knowledge is important for people specializing in bars and similar establishments where well-distributed darkness is used as a design element.

A better, though more cumbersome, method of measuring the effectiveness of lighting systems than by raw footcandles is called equivalent sphere illumination (ESI), which compares actual light readings at a point to a theoretical reading if all the light were delivered from a hemisphere of even brightness, such as the sky. Application of this method is unfortunately not yet perfected.

GLARE

Annoying or even debilitating brightnesses from a fixture or window may shine directly in the eye (direct glare) or may be reflected from the seeing task or nearby surface (indirect or reflected glare). Figure 10.3 indicates the problems.

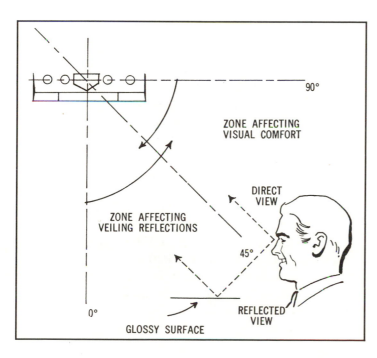

10.3. Visual zones subject to both direct and indirect glare. (*Courtesy of the General Electric Company*)

90°

ZONE AFFECTING
VISUAL COMFORT

DIRECT
VIEW

ZONE AFFECTING
VEILING REFLECTIONS

45°

0°

REFLECTED
VIEW

GLOSSY SURFACE

A simple test for direct glare is to emulate the Indian looking out over the plains and shielding his eyes from the sun with his hand. If you are more comfortable with the hand in place than without it, the fixture is too bright. The cure to this problem is reorientation of either task or fixture (usually not easy) or use of a device providing more light control in the fixture. Parabolic and metal louvers and pigmented lenses are considered the most comfortable such devices, followed by white plastic louvers, clear glass or plastic lenses, and translucent diffusers. Table 10.2 gives a ranking for common control media.

TABLE 10.2. Ranking of fixture control media

Usually comfortable	Less comfortable	Usually uncomfortable
Parabolic wedge louver	Four-lamp, 2 by 4 feet; or two-	Bare lamps
Louvered ceiling	lamp, 1 by 4 feet	
Polarizing material	With poor clear prismatic lens	
Parabolic aluminum troffer	With diffuser	
Suspended fixtures,	Wraparounds	
with 45 by 45 degree		
louvers and opaque or		
dense sides		
Two-lamp, 2- by 4-foot troffer		
with prismatic lens		
Four-lamp, 2 by 4 feet; or		
two-lamp, 1 by 4 feet		
With white louvers		
With good clear prismatic		
lens		

Source: Courtesy of General Electric Company.

Sources of indirect glare, either from conventional office or industrial tasks or from cathode-ray tube screens (see Figures 13.5, 13.6) are not always readily apparent but can often be found by use of a small mirror. Moving the mirror around on the seeing task with the viewer's eye in the normal work position will quickly reveal the offending bright fixture or window. As in correcting for direct glare, relocation of the task or fixture and better light control can alleviate the problem.

Efforts to reduce glare by reduction of light levels are frequent and have limited success; although distracting brightnesses may be reduced, so are brightness and contrast of the task. The result of such attempts is usually a short trial period until a better solution is found. There are "glare-reducing" lamps on the market that do absolutely no good at all. The cure for glare is not in lamp color or light level but in control of brightness from the fixture.

Another attempt to place numbers on lighting quality is the use of visual comfort probability (VCP) tables. Such tables can be calculated by fixture manufacturers from the same data used for coefficient of utilization tables and are often published on catalog sheets. Judicious use of VCP tables allows a designer to forecast whether a given fixture will be obtrusive in a space. The dividing line between comfortable and uncomfortable installations is commonly considered to be 70 percent. A VCP lower than that will result in excessive glare complaints from occupants.

The "perfect" lighting system would be one that allowed all seeing tasks to be performed quickly and easily and in which brightness variations in the field of view were interesting but not obtrusive.

11
GENERAL
APPLICATIONS

LIGHTING DESIGNERS DO NOT WORK IN A VACUUM but must constantly adjust to other space needs. The noise added by ballasts (see Chapter 4) can interfere with testing in a school for the hearing impaired, radio frequencies generated by fluorescent or high-intensity discharge fixtures can cause chaos in electronic manufacturing plants, and infrared from incandescent lamps automatically limits light levels to about 40 footcandles when those sources are used.

The lighting design must relate to basic architectural elements. Perhaps the best illustration of this principle is the 5 by 5 building module that many architects, for very good reasons, fell in love with some years ago. That system dictates that walls and building services be installed on even 5-foot centers in all directions to allow creation of 10- by 10-foot, 15- by 20-foot, and 20- by 20-foot offices or rooms with other dimensions divisible by 5 feet. Lighting fixtures are included in that plan of course and, for visual appropriateness, they should be square, usually 2 feet on each side, as in the office shown in Figure 13.1.

Ceilings, unless they are decorative, are regarded as a necessary evil to be made as inconspicuous as possible. This is particularly significant if the ceiling area is actually ugly, as when industrial or warehouse spaces are converted to residential or commercial use. In addition to construction of a false ceiling below the structural one, a horizontal line can be created around the periphery of the space and everything above that line painted either black or white.

The "paint it black" theory holds that since black, by definition, reflects no light, nothing on the ceiling will be visible. Most spaces treated this way leave visitors with vague expectations of imminent encounters with stalactites and cave-dwelling bats. The "black" method can be made to work by use of black vertical boards in an eggcrate or louver pattern to create a visual ceiling.

The "paint it white" theory maintains that with the whole overhead zone about the same brightness everything up there will disappear. Most space designers prefer, at least once, the "black" solution.

White ceilings are necessary in any design where cost is of primary importance because they produce higher coefficients of utilization and thus require less power and fewer fixtures for a given light level than if a lower reflectance was used. White also contributes to visual comfort by softening shadows and reducing contrasts. Unless other considerations come into play, white should be the only color even considered for ceilings in commercial or industrial applications. However, hospital rooms or dental offices where patients look up for long periods should certainly sacrifice some efficiency by use of lower reflectances in the overhead zone.

Extensive use of white for walls and floors in work spaces should be avoided not only from the maintenance standpoint but for visual comfort as well. An extreme example of misapplication occurred some years ago in a drafting room outside Chicago. The current IESNA recommendation for such areas, 200 maintained footcandles, was followed, with initial levels much higher of course, and the space designer specified white wall coverings and floors.

The first sign of trouble was the loss of several senior draftsmen (there were few women in that job then) by voluntary retirement or resignation. They claimed they could not stand the new quarters. The situation must be visualized to be appreciated. The senior men were all in the choice work positions in the rear of the room looking forward; they all wore white shirts; the drafting tables were covered with white paper; the floor, walls, and doors were all white. All these people could see was white—and bright. A solution of sorts was created by painting some doors and other vertical surfaces with bright colors.

While walls and floors should not ordinarily be white, they should be of relatively high reflectances. Walls in the range of 40 to 60 percent, of any color, are normally acceptable, as are floors reflecting more than 20 percent. In areas of low light levels, say 20 footcandles or less (for example, restaurants), darker walls around 15 or 20 percent reflectance can be tolerated. Use of the space alters the definition of "proper" reflectances. Dark mahogany may not be visually comfortable in conference rooms used for all-day meetings, but, because of its opulent appearance, it is proper in a boardroom where people meet for short periods to discuss handling large amounts of money.

The "feel" of a space can be greatly affected by light distribution from the fixtures. Fluorescent lighting produces a flat, bland atmosphere, the ultimate in that direction being the luminous ceiling, while highly directional downlights cause dramatic contrasts. (In work areas such contrasts are known as reflected glare or harsh shadows.)

Indirect lighting, which means that light is bounced off the ceiling, was provided by incandescent torchiers and floor lamps long before discharge lamps were invented and seems to be making a comeback today. It produces an effect similar to that from a luminous ceiling but is usually more expensive because some light is absorbed by the ceiling no matter how high its reflectance. Indirect systems are slowly reappearing, with reluctant acceptance, in office and store designs. The ambient portion of task/ambient office systems is usually indirect, either from the top of a furniture-mounted fluorescent device, as in Figure 13.4, or from a floor, wall, or suspended high-intensity discharge fixture. See Chapters 13 and 14 for further discussion.

SUMMARY

An important point to remember when faced with a new design problem is that almost every lighting technique can be used in more than one application area. Spotlighting equipment and methods used to highlight merchandise in stores can also be used in residences and public buildings. High-intensity discharge lamps are not limited to industrial areas or parking lots but can also floodlight buildings and illuminate corridors. All sources and techniques should be considered in lighting design.

12 RESIDENCES

MANY OF THE LIGHTING PRINCIPLES USEFUL in residential areas are derived from or are applicable to other spaces. An effective solution should not be rejected for the home just because it is used in foundries or stores. If it works, use it.

Ease and comfort of seeing are as important in living spaces as in work environments. Levels can be a little lower than on the job because of shorter time spent on most tasks, but brightness ratios and potential glare sources should receive the same attention.

The average maintained footcandles or lumen method explained in Chapter 9 is useful in many applications, but do not try it in residences. One reason is that seeing task areas (kitchen counter, desk, bathroom mirror, workbench) are more localized in homes than in work areas. In addition, we should be interested in obtaining more interesting brightness patterns than are created by the formula method.

A simple three-step method has proved quite successful for home lighting designs:

1. Light each specific seeing task. The figures in this chapter illustrate methods.

2. Light each visual focal point (fireplace, picture, spoon rack).

3. Provide ambient, walking-around light in other areas so that there are not any totally dark corners.

The general attributes of high and low lighting levels (controllable by switches and dimmers) apply to residences as well as other spaces. High levels promote a bright, lively atmosphere in homes or cafeterias, while people tend to stay past closing time in dimly lit cocktail lounges or basement bars. Note how fast people get out when you turn on all the lights at the end of a party. Lots of light conveys fast, energetic feelings; low levels induce slow movements.

Ceilings darker than about 60 percent reflectance tend to bring the roof down on people's heads to create a visual cave, while large

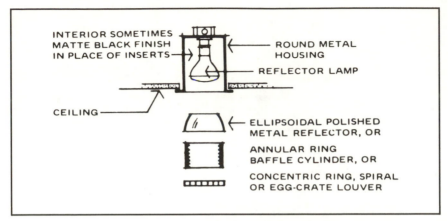

INTERIOR SOMETIMES
MATTE BLACK FINISH
IN PLACE OF INSERTS → ─── ROUND METAL
                              HOUSING

                          ─── REFLECTOR LAMP

CEILING ───

← ELLIPSOIDAL POLISHED
   METAL REFLECTOR, OR

   ANNULAR RING
   BAFFLE CYLINDER, OR

   CONCENTRIC RING, SPIRAL
   OR EGG-CRATE LOUVER

12.1. A typical downlight is shown recessed into the ceiling. They are also available for surface mounting, and, as indicated, with internal reflectors for use with general-service bulbs and other accessories for visual comfort. (*Courtesy of the Illuminating Engineering Society of North America*)

vertical surfaces like draperies and walls are acceptable when between 35 and 60 percent. Darker than that they become heavy and oppressive, while very light walls can become too bright. Floor coverings at 15 to 35 percent reflectance are recommended. White rugs are regarded as rich looking and are fine for small areas, but when too large they can become overly bright.

Downlights (Figure 12.1) fit nicely in dining rooms, over sinks (Figure 12.2), and in living rooms if furniture is not going to be rearranged. Figure 12.3 shows a downlight used to accent a wall-hung item of interest. Recessing such fixtures into the ceilings of existing houses can range from difficult to impossible, depending on construction.

A handy but overused alternative to permanently mounted fixtures like downlights is track lighting and the myriad associated fixtures. Track lighting is great for specific visual tasks (Figure 12.4) and for accent but can provide visual clutter. A simple solution is to hide it behind a cornice (vertical board) finished the same as the ceiling.

Structural fixtures (valances, cornices, brackets), as illustrated in Figures 12.5, 12.6, and 12.7, are very handy for overall illumination with directional sources supplying sparkle, life, and form.

Luminous ceilings work well in kitchens and baths if the structural ceiling is high enough. Intensities in different parts of the room can be varied by switching or by installing different densities of fixtures above the shielding media. Such media, by the way, are

12.2. A downlight (as illustrated) or a fluorescent soffit (as described in Chapter 6) both do a good job of putting light down into the sink. (*Courtesy of Phyllis Boylan*)

12.3. Downlights, as used here, wall-washers, and framing spots can all be used to bring out items of interest in the home. (*Courtesy of Phyllis Boylan*)

12.4. Track lighting, shown here to light a specific task, is a handy alternative to permanently installed fixtures. Fixtures of many shapes and sizes are available to install on the electrified track. (*Courtesy of the General Electric Company*)

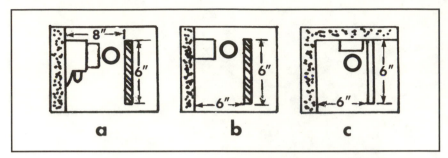

12.5. Suggested dimensions for **(a)** valances, **(b)** wall brackets, and **(c)** cornices. Dimensions should be carefully followed to prevent direct view of the lamp from normal viewing angles. (*Courtesy of the General Electric Company*)

available in many patterns and colors, some even having leaves or butterflies pictured on them. Such panels are merely laid on top of a T-bar grid hung below the structural ceiling.

Portable lamps are quite versatile and, if properly designed, can provide both task and general illumination. The well-engineered ones, however, are not always the most attractive. Figures 6.3 and 12.8 show the problems. Shades that are too tall often require gym-

12.7. A lighted valance in a window corner can supplement daylight on greenery and supply general lighting for the room. Padded drapery material makes an attractive finishing touch. (*Courtesy of Phyllis Boylan*)

LIGHTED CORNICES

Cornices direct all their light downward to give dramatic interest to wall coverings, draperies, murals, etc. May also be used over windows where space above window does not permit valance lighting. Good for low-ceilinged rooms.

VALANCES

Valances are always used at windows, usually with draperies. They provide up-light which reflects off ceiling for general room lighting and down-light for drapery accent. When closer to ceiling than 10 inches use closed top to eliminate annoying ceiling brightness.

WALL BRACKETS (HIGH TYPE)

High wall brackets provide both up and down light for general room lighting. Used on interior walls to balance window valance both architecturally and in lighting distribution. Mounting height determined by window or door height.

WALL BRACKETS (LOW TYPE)

Low brackets are used for special wall emphasis or for lighting specific tasks such as sink, range, reading in bed, etc. Mounting height is determined by eye height of users, from both seated and standing positions. Length should relate to nearby furniture groupings and room scale.

LIGHTED SOFFITS

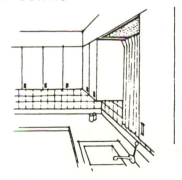

Soffits over work areas are designed to provide higher level of light directly below. Usually they are easily installed in furred-down area over sink in kitchen. Also are excellent for niches over sofas, pianos, built-in desks, etc.

LIGHTED SOFFITS

Bath or dressing room soffits are designed to light user's face. They are almost always used with large mirrors and counter-top lavatories. Length usually tied to size of mirror. Add luxury touch with attractively decorated bottom diffuser.

12.6. Some suggested uses for structural elements. All supply soft, general illumination and should be supplemented by other light sources for specific seeing tasks. (*Courtesy of the Illuminating Engineering Society of North America*)

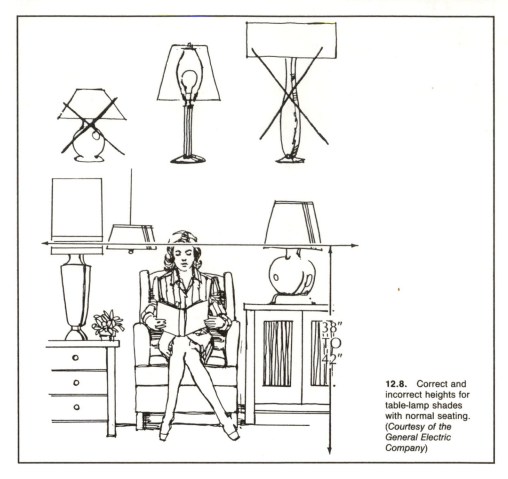

12.8. Correct and incorrect heights for table-lamp shades with normal seating. (*Courtesy of the General Electric Company*)

nastic ability to position reading material in the light, while the very short ones allow view of the bare bulb. The fad of floor lamps with small metal hoods over the light source not only produces uncomfortable pools of light but occasionally hot hoods.

Two fixtures found in most homes are those installed on the back panels of some stoves, throwing absolutely no light into any deep cooking utensil, and picture lights. When the latter are mounted on the bottom of the frame, the fixture itself often blocks the view of the picture; when positioned on top, they result in reflected images of the light source into the viewer's eye. The reflected-image problem can be reduced by nonglare glass but can be eliminated by the method used in galleries. As illustrated in Figure 12.9, light sources out of the reflected field of view will illuminate, yet their brightness will not obscure, the object being viewed.

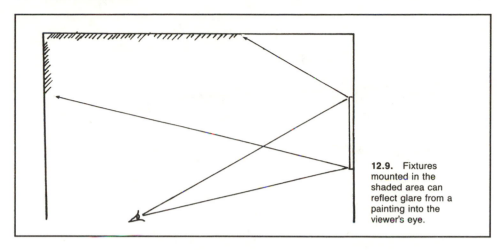

12.9. Fixtures mounted in the shaded area can reflect glare from a painting into the viewer's eye.

KITCHENS

Perhaps the area of a home in which the most difficult prolonged seeing tasks take place is the kitchen. Food preparation, color and texture judgment during the cooking process, and the unavoidable cleanup all require prolonged observation with enough light of the right color. Use of cool white and, earlier, daylight colors in bare-lamp kitchen fixtures is the main reason fluorescent lamps are anathema today for most homemakers who feel, understandably but incorrectly, that fluorescent lighting has to be bright, harsh, and ugly.

General light in a kitchen is best provided by a ceiling-mounted fixture, either fluorescent or incandescent, in the center of the room. Common types are shown in Figure 12.10. They could be about 150 watts of incandescent (remember that two 75s do not give as much light as one 150) or 80 watts of fluorescent. Used alone, such a fixture will cause shadows on tasks around the periphery of the room. Another excellent source is a luminous ceiling.

Sinks need light, the fixture usually recessed in a soffit. Undercabinet lights are the way to get rid of the body-caused shadow on the food-preparation area. The most efficient ones must be hardwired (not just plugged into a convenience outlet) and feature replaceable lamps, while the more convenient types are mounted on the underside of the cabinet with a couple of screws and then plugged into an outlet. Either type should be mounted at the front of the cabinet rather than at the back and should be shielded from the view of people seated in the area.

12.10. Kitchens require a large central light, with others for the sink, cabinets, and counters. Note the under-cabinet light to illuminate the work area. These should be well shielded from seated viewing. (*Courtesy of the General Electric Company*)

BATHROOM

Face lighting over the sink or at a makeup mirror should be done with one large source or a number of small sources to cast light on all parts of the face and reduce shadows to a minimum. An old standard method of mounting tubular incandescent lamps on each side of the mirror does a pretty good job of this, but the bulbs are very inefficient, expensive, and subject to breakage every time the cabinet door is slammed.

The dressing-room approach with globular incandescent lamps around the edge of the mirror (Figure 12.11) works only if too high a wattage and thus brightness is not used. The same caution applies when using table lamps, as in Figure 12.12.

An open-topped soffit above the sink floods the face evenly, with the light out the top of the fixture providing general illumination. Visibility under the chin for shaving comes from light bounced off a high-reflectance sink.

The perfect color light for makeup application does not exist any more than it does for choice of paint, wall coverings, or fabrics.

78" TO FLOOR

12.11. Many fixtures work well over bathroom or makeup mirrors as long as they direct light to the face from several directions. (*Courtesy of the General Electric Company*)

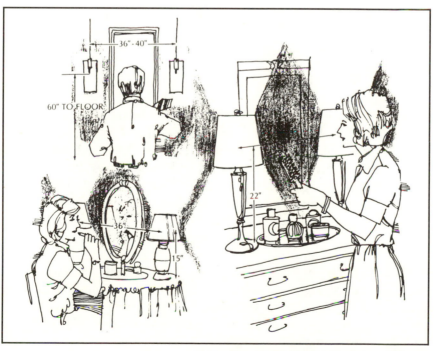

36" - 40"

60" TO FLOOR

22"

36"

15"

12.12. Personal grooming requires long or widely spaced sources to cast light on each side of the face. (*Courtesy of the General Electric Company*)

Makeup effects applied under incandescent light will fade under the widely used cool white or warm white fluorescent colors because there is less red light emitted by them than by the incandescent. The face that looked fine in the office bathroom can become garish under incandescent light at the bar after work. The only sure way, not easy, to be certain makeup will look right under all conditions is to inspect it both under very blue light (cool white fluorescent) and then under very red light (incandescent).

OTHER AREAS

Dining areas probably need more versatility in lighting than any other space in a residence. Board games are played, correspondence carried on, meetings held, and meals consumed, each of which requires different lighting levels and atmospheres. Bulk ambient light can be supplied by valances, coves, wall sconces, or any of the structural methods, with a chandelier on a dimmer to provide the proper sparkle and richness and perhaps downlights or track fixtures for judicious spotlighting.

Chandeliers should be mentioned because they are so widely used, primarily in dining rooms. As a task light, they are often lamped with too high a wattage and become overly bright. As a source of sparkle with use of low-wattage lamps, they are fine. Operation on dimmers allows variations of brightness and light level for different functions.

Ironing, a home task with special needs, can be lighted very nicely with a fluorescent worklight mounted slightly in front of the ironing board. Do not keep the cool white lamps normally provided; trade them in for one of the better colors discussed in Chapter 4.

As anyone who has ever sewed on dark cloth with dark thread can testify, sewing is perhaps the most difficult seeing task in the home. In fact, it is about 100 times as difficult to see as normal office tasks. Sewing machine manufacturers have helped with machine lights, but restrictions of space and location limit their effectiveness. High-intensity lamps and spotlights are useful for the small areas involved.

Extended studying has different needs than casual reading. Light levels should be higher and greater care taken to eliminate shadows and glare. Either two portable lamps, one on each side of the study surface, or a suitably placed fluorescent fixture (Figure 12.13) will do an adequate job.

12.13. Study areas contain one of the most critical seeing tasks in the home. (*Courtesy of the General Electric Company*)

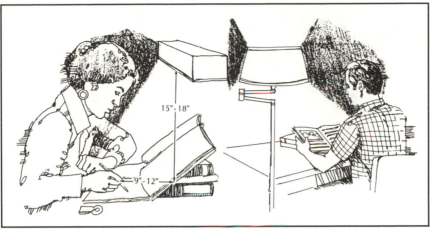

OUTDOOR

Outdoor lighting can extend enjoyment of a home immeasurably. Anything more complicated than substitution of a yellow bug light in an existing fixture, however, requires planning for the proper effect. Lighting on just one or two trees, shrubs, or flower patches in a setting can achieve a spectacular effect. Low-voltage lighting strings are fine for this purpose, as are 120-volt spots and floods when safely installed.

A common method of lighting trees is from the ground (Figure 12.14), but a very acceptable and more theatrical way is to aim lights

12.14. Lighted trees extend enjoyment of the outdoor view into evening and nighttime hours. As with any lighting system, the bright lamp should be shielded from view. (*Courtesy of the General Electric Company*)

12.15. Tree-mounted fixtures create interesting shadows and a moonlight effect on the ground. (*Courtesy of the General Electric Company*)

down from somewhere up in the tree (Figure 12.15). The higher the source, the less obvious and more effective it is.

Foliage is greatly enhanced by blue or green PAR lamps, particularly the dichroic variety, and by clear mercury. Fir trees become even more beautiful when illuminated with clear mercury lamps. Mercury lamp and fixture costs, however, have limited their use.

Summer festivities can be greatly enlivened by lighted plastic bubbles or lanterns in the party area or by clamp-on lights aimed into the underside of beach umbrellas. The bug problem might be alleviated by asking the neighbors to turn on some high-wattage bulbs for the evening.

PLANT GROWTH LIGHTS

Many plants can be propagated and grown quite successfully in home growth chambers. Normal watering and feeding practices should be followed, with fluorescent lamps providing the necessary light. Figure 12.16 shows light levels resulting from a two-lamp fluorescent work light. The 400 or 500 footcandles about a foot below the fixture are about the same level as experienced outdoors in the shade of a tree. Since light is additive, more lamps can be used until the desired level is reached.

Home hobbyists with a space problem can construct their own growth unit (Figure 12.17) or buy one of the many available at garden shops. The purple-appearing "growth" lamps usually seen in these stores will aid growth all right, but not as much as higher lumen lamps like cool white or warm white. They also cost more than most other colors.

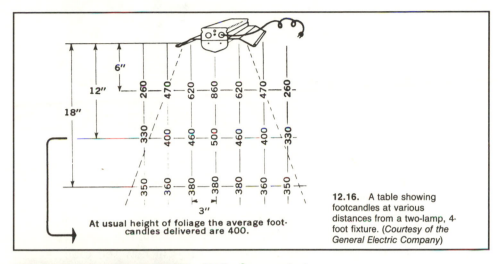

12.16. A table showing footcandles at various distances from a two-lamp, 4-foot fixture. (*Courtesy of the General Electric Company*)

12.17. One example of a home-designed and home-built growth fixture. Many other types are available commercially. (*Courtesy of the General Electric Company*)

SUMMARY

The miniscule amount of lighting equipment installed by home builders and apartment owners requires that more be supplied by the resident. Besides portable lamps, there are many very attractive fluorescent and incandescent fixtures for ceiling or wall mounting and a great variety of track-mounted fixtures. Many of these can be seen in showrooms or catalogs. Homes do not have to be dark.

13
OFFICES

OFFICE LIGHTING IS STILL IN THE THROES of the energy "crisis, crunch, emergency," or whatever occurred in the early seventies when OPEC cut down the flow of oil and raised prices so dramatically. The panic resulting from those moves has resulted in lowered light levels through lamp removal, fewer fixtures in new space designs, and widespread use of low-energy (sometimes low-light) lamps and ballasts. Electrical usage for lighting has dropped, but costs have not kept pace because of rising electrical rates. Heroes of industry have emerged from decreased energy spending (cost dollars are easy to find), but resultant losses from increased errors and lowered productivity caused by decreased visibility are not immediately apparent. Wholesale reductions in light levels for work areas should be viewed with suspicion until it is certain that worker efficiency will not suffer.

SEEING TASKS

Anyone not closely involved might assume that office seeing tasks, other than video screens, involve only typewritten reading matter, while in reality poorly duplicated copies (carbons, copy machines), illegible phone-line transmissions, nearly undecipherable handwriting in hard pencil, and the last copy from a multipart form are much more prevalent. The problem of handling these communications is made even more difficult by low light levels, direct and reflected glare, and excessive brightness differences between the task and its visual background. White paper seen against rich (read "dark") office furniture just does not fit into the recommended brightness ratios.

Any uniform pattern of fixtures (Figures 13.1, 13.2, 13.3) will result in some of those fixtures falling into a worker's reflected field of view. Often the specific cause of "glare, too bright, eye strain," and similar complaints can be identified (see Chapter 10) by place-

13.1. The 5-by-5 module popular for office buildings, in which all services and partition supports are installed 5 feet apart in a grid pattern, engendered the 2- by 2-foot fixture shown here. They contain either two or three **U**-tube fluorescent lamps. (*Courtesy of the General Electric Company*)

13.2. Complete ceiling systems including air-handling equipment, acoustical material, sprinklers, and lighting fixtures have lost popularity despite their high visual comfort. Note how fixture brightness disappears at relatively low viewing angles. (*Courtesy of the General Electric Company*)

13.3. 150-watt high-pressure sodium lamps in 2- by 2-foot troffers, as shown here, result in an adequate light level but in fixture brightness that becomes uncomfortable. (*Courtesy of the General Electric Company*)

ment of a small pocket mirror on the seeing task, whether it is paper on a work surface or information on a video screen. When neither the offending fixture nor the seeing task can be moved to eliminate glare, use of a more comfortable shielding device on the fixture often works. The best of these devices is the parabolic wedge louver which should normally be the first cure considered for video complaints. See Table 10.2 for a comfort ranking of light control media.

SPACE REQUIREMENTS

When other considerations are not paramount, surfaces in offices should meet the following reflectance criteria for best seeing comfort: ceilings, 80 to 90 percent; walls, 40 to 60 percent; furniture, 25 to 45 percent; machines, 25 to 45 percent; and floors, 20 to 40 percent. Drastic departures from these recommendations can cause client unhappiness and possible delayed payment for services.

Because specific office layouts are usually unknown during construction, speculative buildings require an overall lighting system that can be adapted to any space requirement. Such uniform patterns, however, often result in too little light for some areas and too much for others. Solutions are imaginative switching to vary light levels with use and installation of flexible power whips, where allowed by local code, to allow relocation of fixtures.

FIXTURES

Far and away the most common office fixture used today is the four-lamp, 2- by 4-foot troffer with a prismatic lens for control. Anyone using lowest cost per fixture as the primary criterion will end up buying these equipped with standard ballasts and 40-watt cool white lamps. Often the quality of ballasts, maintenance devices such as hinges and latches, and steel, has been sacrificed to reach such competitive prices. Variations in size, such as 1 by 4 feet or 2 by 2 feet (Figure 13.1) do not do much to change the basic problem of fixtures that are too bright. Prismatic lenses just cannot control glare well enough to be totally comfortable in offices.

As discussed in Chapter 10, fixture brightness is usually reduced when louvers are substituted for lenses. Small parabolic wedge louvers provide almost perfect control of direct glare but are rather expensive. The currently popular large-cell parabolics have encountered the inevitable clash with costs by becoming shallower and thus less effective.

OTHER SYSTEMS

Other office lighting systems in limited use today are suspended direct-indirect fixtures that are quite comfortable but disappearing because of lower ceiling heights, luminous ceilings (Chapter 6), and coffered ceiling systems like that in Figure 13.2. Two-foot-square troffers holding 150-watt high-pressure sodium (HPS) lamps (Figure 13.3) have been tried, but fixture brightness is quite high. One notorious installation went into a northeastern school using 250-watt HPS lamps in similar fixtures but was removed because of justified public uproar. However, the media blamed the bad installation on lamp color rather than on fixture brightness.

Wraparounds are sometimes used in renovations but, as noted in Chapter 6, have sides that are far too bright for normal office use. They are cheaper than more comfortable fixtures and, for some reason, always seem to be in distributor stock.

The trendy general fluorescent system today features one- or two-lamp lensed or open-topped cylinders suspended horizontally a foot or so below the ceiling. These come in a variety of colors and, like any indirect system, are quite satisfactory at relatively low foot-candle levels. Too many of them in a space, however, can cause overly bright ceilings and a visual forest of fixtures and hangers.

Task/ambient office lighting, a darling of many designers, came into vogue in the seventies as an energy-saving method and is still evolving. The ambient, or walking-around, part can be provided by conventional ceiling-mounted units, indirect metal halide fixtures, or the same fixtures providing the task light. Task light is usually now supplied by one or more fluorescent lamps mounted in precisely the worst position—at the front of the work station near eye level, as in Figure 13.4. Lamps are usually shielded from direct view by baffles or lenses, but these do not eliminate glare reflected from the task or desk. Footcandle readings taken at the work position will be high but will not reveal the resultant indirect glare.

13.4. A task/ambient lighting system with the ambient portion sup-plied by uplight from the desk-mounted task lights. (*Courtesy of the General Electric Company*)

Indirect high-intensity discharge fixtures for ambient lighting contain a 250- or 400-watt metal halide lamp and can be floor, ceiling, or partition mounted. Some are equipped with an adjustable opening on the bottom to provide downlight on the task. In theory, the uplight supplies sufficient ambient light, and judicious placement of fixtures furnishes light on the task from at least two directions. In practice, desk lamps are often seen at work stations because the indirect component is not enough to work by and annoying shadows can result from too few sources. Workers have been known to steal fixtures (most are portable) from other locations to get enough light at their own work stations. Creative accounting can sometimes provide tax benefits by writing off the portable fixtures as furniture rather than as part of the building.

Open office plans, often using more floor space than traditional layouts, become even more wasteful when floor-standing indirect lighting fixtures are used. Not only does the fixture take up expensive square feet, the ceiling soaks up at least 20 percent of the light generated. In its favor, indirect lighting is usually quite comfortable, at least at low levels, and is a solution to the video tube problem where the video display terminal is the only visual task involved. Group relamping of such metal halide systems is quite important because lamps change color with burning time and a mixture of old and new lamps can give the ceiling an uneven appearance.

5-BY-5 MODULE

Several years ago the architectural concept known as the 5-by-5 module came into existence for office buildings and spawned a whole new lighting system—the 2- by 2-foot fixture illustrated in Figure 13.1. This modular approach places all services (electric lines, phone wires, wall-support systems, light fixtures) in a 5-foot grid pattern. Individual offices can then measure 10 by 10 feet, 10 by 15, or any size desired as long as they are in some multiple of 5 feet. More conventional and cheaper, 2- by 4-foot rectangular fixtures would physically fit in the module but would look strange if they ended up situated crosswise in corridors, so square fixtures were desired for appearance.

Two-foot lamps of 20 watts were the only ones then available that would fit comfortably into the desired 2- by 2-foot fixture, but it would be very expensive because of the number of lamps needed (at least four to get a decent light level) and attendant sockets and ballasts. The solution was the U-tube, 4 feet in length and bent back on itself to fit nicely into the 2-foot fixture (see Figure 6.2).

THE GREAT VIDEO CONTROVERSY

Perhaps the biggest problem in the lighting world today is the proper illumination of offices and other work areas containing video screens. The traditional tasks of preparing and interpreting information on paper are fast disappearing and being replaced by the same work on video display terminals. The more common reasons for direct and reflected glare are shown in Figure 13.5.

13.5. Uncomfortable screen viewing can be caused by direct glare from fixtures or windows or by reflected brightness of fixtures, windows, or the operator's clothing. (*Courtesy of the General Electric Company*)

An occasionally successful approach is to treat the screen itself. Nonglare shields on the screen help with reflected glare, but their name promises a bit more than is delivered. Different background color of the screen seems to be a matter of individual choice rather than a glare solution. Hoods are available to obscure some of the causes of direct and reflected glare.

The first solution usually offered for correcting the glare problem is an indirect lighting system (Figure 13.4). The whole ceiling thus becomes approximately the same brightness, and screen intensity can be adjusted to wash out the overall brightness. This works fine up to about 40 footcandles, whereupon ceiling brightness, while even, becomes too bright. Illumination levels below 40 footcandles are all right when most of the operator's time is spent looking at the screen but can cause fatigue if much paper is involved. It should be remembered that many people with a computer or other video terminal at their work stations still do a great deal of old-fashioned paperwork.

Another method for solving video problems is use of low-brightness parabolic louvers in direct fixtures. The louvers drastically reduce both direct and reflected glare and allow a comfortable light level on traditional seeing tasks. Care in choice of such louvers is important, however, because the most comfortable ones are also the most expensive. In this case (as detailed in Chapter 10) cheaper also usually means brighter.

Light fixtures are not the only glare sources. Windows, pictures (Figure 13.6), bulletin boards, and even the worker's clothing (Figure 13.5) can all be bright enough to obscure information on the screen. Blinds or draperies can be installed on windows, pictures moved or removed, and (with dictatorial overtones) dress codes established to alleviate clothing problems.

13.6. Even though the fixtures are equipped with low-brightness parabolic wedge louvers, glare problems persist from the uncontrolled window and poster brightnesses. (*Courtesy of the General Electric Company*)

PRIVATE OFFICES

In private offices, light levels are usually highest in the center, where the occupant may seldom work. Lighting in private offices should first be designed for the work areas (desk, credenza, conference table); then the rest of the room should be treated to provide ambient light and reduce brightness contrasts. Video tasks should be considered along with the other chores of the executive. A very handy tool for brightening the usually dark wall opposite the desk is a fluorescent wall bracket. Table lamps can be spotted around the room to soften the atmosphere and reduce contrasts.

SUMMARY

The change in office seeing tasks from paper to electronic information exchange requires corresponding changes in lighting solutions. The reactionary designer who does not keep up with that change will encounter a decreasing share of the available contracts.

14
STORES AND OTHER APPLICATIONS

THIS CHAPTER WILL NOT ANSWER all the lighting questions encountered in stores, restaurants, schools, banks, hospitals and other commercial spaces. It will discuss some special problems in each application area and suggest some general solutions.

STORES

Store lighting allows more imaginative solutions than any other application, with the exception of the arts. An effective design must not only provide light for the seeing tasks of both customer and employee but should also have a theatrical, show-biz quality to it. Too many store specifiers get carried away with their own designs and lose track of the fact that the main reason for a lighting system is to allow customers to see the merchandise.

Lighting can help shoppers know that soup is down that aisle or coats on this rack and then helps them to distinguish among brands, flavors, sizes, prices, and colors. Fixture patterns can help lead people in desired directions, and well-planned brightness differences can point to key displays. Properly used, they can augment the atmosphere and architectural elements of the space. Even outside lighting comes into play by giving the store or mall the appearance of being a safe, pleasant place to spend money. Entrances are identified by sign displays, distinguishing architectural features, and high brightnesses.

Three separate lighting systems are required to fully present the merchandise, the decor, and the structure of a store. These are general lighting, distributed fairly uniformly over the store, vertical lighting on the upper walls, and spotlighting of feature displays.

The first of these, normally fluorescent, provides the bulk of the proper-color footcandles for adequate appraisal of merchandise. Either ignorance of available fluorescent colors or blind adherence to a footcandle standard while striving for low initial and operating costs has caused many store operators to forget the color aspect. The newer phosphors at various color temperatures make it possible to maintain desired light levels at low costs while gaining the benefits of excellent color rendition.

Light levels used by high-volume self-service stores usually fall into the 60- to 100-footcandle range, with only a few remaining above 100. Department, specialty, and "exclusive" stores often get along with levels as low as 20. Those light readings, usually taken on a horizontal plane in the center of an aisle, do not really indicate how much light is on the merchandise displayed vertically at the side of the aisle. Vertical footcandles in areas uniformly lighted with bare-lamp fluorescent fixtures or lensed troffers are about 60 percent of horizontal readings.

There are several valid reasons for mass merchandisers to use surface-mounted, bare-lamp fluorescent strip fixtures for general lighting. It is an inexpensive-looking system, which implies to the shopper that overhead costs are low; it proclaims to passersby that the store is open, and because light goes out in all directions, it does a pretty good job on walls and other vertical surfaces. The problem with bare lamps is that they are the brightest object in the shopper's field of view and thus visually detract from the merchandise.

Troffers, usually 2 by 4 feet, are also quite common, do a decent job on vertical surfaces, and appear classier than bare lamps; although they too are usually the brightest objects in the store. When more comfortable and expensive light-control devices such as parabolic louvers are used, vertical surfaces suffer because they direct most of the light downward.

Store lighting with mercury and metal halide lamps has been tried in the past, either in downlights (Figure 14.1) or in square fixtures, with only limited acceptance. No matter how good the color-rendering properties of the high-intensity discharge (HID) lamp, some merchandise just looks different than we think it should. Fabrics are particularly vulnerable to color shifts. The newer 3000 degree Kelvin metal halide sources seem to offer some hope for HID in merchandising, but they are not yet fully accepted.

A second system, also usually fluorescent, brightens the upper walls around the periphery of the space. These bright surfaces show that the store is open, visually expand the space, and often contain graphics to identify areas of the store. Many stores supply this verti-

14.1. Downlights containing either mercury or metal halide lamps had a brief fling of popularity for general store lighting, but most such systems have returned to fluorescent. Low fixture brightness, sparkle on the merchandise, and high vertical footcandles were positive features of these high-intensity discharge downlights, while color distortion and deep shadowing were negatives. (*Courtesy of the General Electric Company*)

cal light from valances or coves along the wall, and where clothing is sold, the same valances can light the garment display. Space considerations often cause the valances to be positioned too close to the wall, resulting in copious light on the garment shoulders, which are out of view, and little light on the sleeves, greater portions of which are displayed (Figure 14.2). A troublesome side effect of lamps mounted very close to fabrics is fading, caused somewhat by ultraviolet but mainly by light.

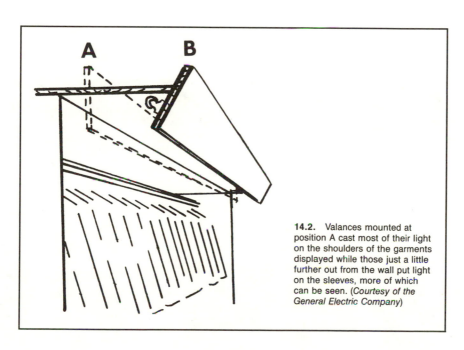

14.2. Valances mounted at position A cast most of their light on the shoulders of the garments displayed while those just a little further out from the wall put light on the sleeves, more of which can be seen. (*Courtesy of the General Electric Company*)

The third lighting system, currently incandescent, is used to spotlight displays and provide sparkle for shiny goods. Brightness differences on the order of five times the surrounding areas are required to attract the attention of shoppers, although the bright area need not be very large. Spotlighting has traditionally been done with relatively inexpensive PAR and R lamps, but more efficient low-voltage quartz lamps, called MR-16, are becoming increasingly popular. They are not much more efficient as measured by lumens per watt, but because of very small filaments and better reflector control, they do a better job of delivering light where it is needed. See the full discussion of these lamps in Chapter 4.

Displays visible from outside the store, whether in formal show windows (Figure 14.3), or at the front of mall stores, must compete with reflections in the glass. Those facing streets vie with reflected images of vehicles, buildings, and facing competitors. People often stop in front of show windows to adjust hair and clothing because that glass makes a great mirror. Displays reflecting 50 percent of the light falling on them must receive 500 or more footcandles even to be noticed through the reflected images. The normal way of achieving that high a light level is to use narrow-beam incandescent equipment, such as low-voltage PAR or MR-16 lamps on a small portion of the display.

14.3. Unless several hundred footcandles of general lighting and a thousand or more of spotlighting are supplied in exterior show windows, reflected images of cars, buildings, and the competitor across the street will obstruct the view of the merchandise. (*Courtesy of the General Electric Company*)

Glass-topped display cases present special problems. Downlights reflected in the top can obscure merchandise if the fixtures are positioned over the center or rear of the case. Proper placement above the customer's side eliminates the problem. Cases lighted from the inside, with either fluorescent or incandescent, result in lamps positioned close to or even touching the merchandise. Since fading of pigments results primarily from the product of light level times time, products not rotated regularly soon become unsalable. No magic ultraviolet-absorbing lamp or filter will eliminate this problem. The only solution is either rapid movement of merchandise or no light.

RESTAURANTS

While lighting of restaurants is often a design decision rather than one dictated by seeing tasks, several principles should be borne in mind. As in any space, high light levels promote activity, so provide plenty of light for high turnover of customers. Check your favorite successful fast food outlet to see this tenet in action. If, on the other hand, the owner wants people to linger, feel unhurried, and, perhaps have that extra drink, the lighting should be "soft," meaning low brightnesses and footcandle readings. Such low lighting levels, however, provide a problem for reading the menu and for the people cleaning up the next morning. And many restaurants want a different atmosphere at noon than at night. The solution is to provide versatility with either more than one lighting system or controls so that the level can be changed. Downlights on dimmers are very handy for this purpose.

Many restaurants use yellow or amber lights because the operator feels those colors create a warm, friendly atmosphere. They may make people feel better, and that is open to discussion, but they also change the color of the food, which may not be so good. The effect is similar to the classic "Turn on the blue lights, Sam, the man wants a blue suit."

SCHOOLS

One of the differences between classrooms and other reading-oriented spaces is that the occupants, other than the instructor, are all facing in the same direction. This allows fixture orientation and placement for maximum visual comfort. Another is that a great deal of the student's time is spent looking at or above the horizontal, making fixture brightness even more important than usual. Displays at the front of the room, including chalkboards, can be made much more visible by a separate chalkboard lighting system.

Increased use of audiovisual teaching aids (movies, slides, television) has necessitated lighting systems that can be altered by switching or dimming to keep light off the vertical screen while providing horizontal illumination for reading and note taking. The usual approach is a separately switched and dimmed downlighting arrangement in addition to the fluorescent fixtures.

Cathode-ray tube or video screens present the same visual problems they do in offices, namely, obscuring of visual information by reflected brightnesses on the glass of the screen. The solutions are low-brightness fixtures (not low light output but low brightness) and uniform vertical brightness of other visible surfaces. This issue is discussed more fully in Chapter 13.

Study carrels can be likened to office work stations in that the vertical elements of each cut off illumination except from limited directions and that most of the current lighting solutions depend on a fluorescent fixture in the perfect position to create reflected glare—straight in front of the user. Downlights for general lighting in carrel areas cause extremely harsh shadows and should be avoided.

Book stacks in school and other libraries remain one of the most difficult areas to light effectively. The problem is one of providing adequate light on vertical surfaces in a long, narrow space, using only the ceiling for fixture mounting. In practice, the lower shelves of most libraries are usually dark. The best solution to date is use of fluorescent fixtures that are specially designed for stacks (Figures 9.5, 14.4).

Daylighting has long been depended upon to augment, if not actually supplant, electrical illumination in schools. It is free, thus appealing to school boards, and also natural, thereby somehow healthier for our children. Architects have always been fascinated with its form-revealing directional character (when the sun is shining) and color. The facts that it is available only half the time (even less during the school year), that it provides adequate light only near the window, and that its brightness must be properly controlled by shades or blinds are all usually glossed over. The result of such short-sighted planning too often results in underlighted classrooms with horrible glare from the uncontrolled windows.

14.4. The difficult lighting task on book stacks is best solved by use of fixtures specifically designed for that use, but they are more expensive than many other fixtures. (*Courtesy of Lighting Products, Inc.*)

BANKS

The public areas of banks must have working light at stand-up desks for customer use in addition to a general system. Supplementary fixtures at those desks are often the best solution.

Teller stations and adjacent work areas are separated from the public space, and the lighting should so indicate. Dropped ceilings with distinctive shielding devices in the fixtures are often used. Seeing tasks here are the same as in other offices, consisting of data manipulation on paper and video display screens, handwriting interpretation, and general paperwork.

Private offices, such as those used by the various vice-presidents for conferences, should exude money, responsibility, trustworthiness, and all the other desirable traits of the banking community. Subdued, inconspicuous lighting systems, which should be dimmer controlled, can help give the proper impression to the customer, who often may be wary.

Drive-up windows and their adjacent teller stations present a special problem in that the teller should be able to see the customer's face. The top of the car can cast a shadow on that face, however, if care is not taken. The easiest solution would be to shine lights along the teller's line of sight, but that would blind the customers. The solution is to place fixtures so that light covering the customer's face comes in under the top of the car window but is no lower than 45 degrees above the horizontal. This placement simultaneously provides light for the customer to fill out forms.

HOSPITALS

Many areas of hospitals should be treated no differently than similar spaces in other buildings. The lobbies, kitchens, gift shops, stairwells, and many storage and work rooms could be in any office building.

Corridors in health care facilities require two levels of lighting—one for daytime use and a lower one when patients are sleeping. The fixtures cannot merely be turned off, since the medical personnel need light to get around. Controls should be located at the nurses station.

Patient rooms are best served with four different systems: (1) a general system, often indirect (for casual use, visitors, television viewing), (2) a reading light for each bed, (3) an examination light for medical personnel (these are often portable and moved from room to room) and (4) a night light.

Lighting of nurses stations is vital. There should be plenty of local controls installed to allow medical personnel to fine-tune the system to their own needs. At the very least they require a day and a night level. Medical records must be well illuminated where they are found so they do not have to be moved to a better location for reading. New and remodeled stations abound in video tubes and should be treated the same as if they were in offices. See Chapter 13 for details.

COMMERCIAL AREAS

Lighting in museums, public buildings, and other commercial areas is most often approached with only architectural or design concepts in mind and with very little thought given to performance of seeing tasks. A frequent result is that soon after opening, a makeshift lighting system is tried and later, at great expense, an adequate one is installed. The careful designer will thoroughly evaluate the actual seeing tasks to be encountered before tackling any such installation.

SUMMARY

While the application shown in Figure 14.5 is certainly not modern or glamorous, it epitomizes the principles of the perfect lighting solution. The simplified approach listed below will work in even the most complex situation:

1. Identify the seeing tasks and design for the proper light levels.
2. Choose a light source for efficiency, color, control requirements, and any other important criteria.
3. Select a fixture with desired light control, appearance, and maintenance characteristics.
4. Provide sufficient controls for occupant flexibility of light levels with changing task locations.

14.5. The lighting in this parking garage does its job effectively without glare and, using high-pressure sodium lamps, is highly energy efficient and cost effective. (*Courtesy of the General Electric Company*)

APPENDIX | LAMP CATALOG

TABLE A.1. Incandescent lamps

Bulb size	Base	Ordering abbreviation	Volts	Description	Life (hours)	Initial lumens	Lumens per watt
S-6	Cand	3S6/5	120	Clear—indicator	3,000	12	4
S-6	Cand	6S6	120	Clear—indicator	1,500	41	7
C-7	Cand	7C7	120	Clear—indicator	3,000	46	7
S-11	Med	7½S	120	Clear—indicator	1,400	53	7
S-14	Med	11S14	130	Clear—sign	3,000	80	7
S-14	Med	11S14/B	130	Blue—sign	3,000	...	...
S-14	Med	11S14/G	130	Green—sign	3,000	...	...
S-14	Med	11S14/O	130	Orange—sign	3,000	...	...
S-14	Med	11S14/R	130	Red—sign	3,000	...	...
S-14	Med	11S14/W	130	White—sign	3,000	59	5
S-14	Med	11S14/Y	130	Yellow—sign	3,000	51	5
S-14	Med	11S14/TB	130	Transparent blue	3,000	...	...
S-14	Med	11S14/TG	130	Transparent green	3,000	...	...
S-14	Med	11S14/TO	130	Transparent orange	3,000	...	...
S-14	Med	11S14/TR	130	Transparent red	3,000	...	...
S-14	Med	11S14/TY	130	Transparent yellow	3,000	...	...
A-15	Med	15A/W	120	White	2,500	120	8
B-10	Cand	15BC	120	Clear—decorative	1,500	136	9
CA-8	Cand	15CAC	120	Clear—bent tip	1,500	...	...
F-10	Cand	15FC	120	Clear—decorative	1,500	136	9
F-10	Cand	15FC/A	120	Amber—decorative	1,500	...	...
G-16	Cand	15GC	120	Clear—decorative	1,500	130	9
T-7	Inter	15T7/N	120	Clear—appliance	...	108	7
A-15	Med	15A/B	120	Blue	2,500	...	...
A-15	Med	15A/G	120	Green	2,500	...	...
A-15	Med	15A/O	120	Orange	2,500	...	...
A-15	Med	15A/R	120	Red	2,500	...	...
A-15	Med	15A/Y	120	Yellow	2,500	...	...
A-19	Med	25A/W	120	White	2,500	190	8
B-10	Cand	25BC	120	Clear—decorative	1,500	...	...
B-10	Cand	25BC/W	120	White—decorative	1,500	...	...
B-13	Med	25BM/W	120	White—decorative	1,500	...	...
CA-10	Cand	25CAC	120	Clear—bent tip	1,500	...	...
ST-10	Cand	25STC	120	Clear—straight tip	1,500	...	...
F-15	Med	25FM	120	Clear—decorative	1,500	240	10
F-10	Cand	25FC	120	Clear—decorative	1,500	...	...
G-16	Cand	25GC	120	Clear—decorative	1,500	235	9
G-16	Cand	25GC/W	120	White—decorative	1,500	210	8
G-18	Med	25G18/W	120	White—decorative	1,500	220	9
G-25	Med	25G25	120	Clear—decorative	1,500	240	10
G-25	Med	25G25/W	120	White—decorative	1,500	220	9
G-40	Med	25G40/W	120	White—decorative	2,500	150	6
G-25	Med	25G40	120	Clear—decorative	2,500	160	6
A-19	Med	25A/B	120	Blue—decorative	2,500	...	...
A-19	Med	25A/G	120	Green—decorative	2,500	...	...
A-19	Med	25A/O	120	Orange—decorative	2,500	...	...
A-19	Med	25A/R	120	Red—decorative	2,500	...	...
A-19	Med	25A/TB	120	Transparent blue	2,500	...	...
A-19	Med	25A/TG	120	Transparent green	2,500	...	...
A-19	Med	25A/TO	120	Transparent orange	2,500	...	...
A-19	Med	25A/TR	120	Transparent red	2,500	...	...
A-19	Med	25ATY	120	Transparent yellow	2,500	...	...
T-6	Int	25T6	120	Clear—showcase	1,000	244	10
T-8	Int	25T8DC	120	Clear—appliance	...	195	8

Note: Cand = candelabra, Med = medium, Inter = intermediate, SC bay = single-contact bayonet, DC bay = double-contact bayonet.

TABLE A.1. (*Continued*)   **Incandescent lamps**

Bulb size	Base	Ordering abbreviation	Volts	Description	Life (hours)	Initial lumens	Lumens per watt
T-10	Med	25T10	120	Clear—showcase	1,000	248	10
PAR-36	Screw	25PAR36	5.5	PAR—very narrow spot	1,000	...	...
PAR-46	Screw	25PAR46	5.5	PAR—very narrow spot	1,000	...	...
R-20	Med	30R20	120	Reflector—flood	2,000	210	7
A-21	3-contact med	30/100	120	3-Way—white	1,500	1,315	13
A-19	Med	40A/W	120	White	1,500	440	11
A-15	Med	40A15	120	Appliance—oven	1,500	455	11
B-10	Cand	40BC	120	Clear—decorative	1,500	...	...
B-13	Med	40BM	120	Clear—decorative	1,500	455	11
PAR-38	Med	45PAR/SP/H	120	Halogen spot	2,000	...	...
PAR-38	Med	45PAR/FL/H	120	Halogen flood	2,000	...	...
PAR-38	Med	45PAR/NSP/H	120	Halogen narrow spot	2,000	...	...
R-20	Med	50R20/FL	120	Reflector—flood	2,000	440	9
PAR-36	Screw	50PAR36/NSP	12	PAR—narrow spot	2,000	...	...
PAR-36	Screw	50PAR36/WFL	12	PAR—wide flood	2,000	...	...
PAR-36	Screw	50PAR36/VWF	12	PAR—very wide flood	2,000	...	...
A-21	3-contact med	50/150	120	3-Way—white	1,500	2,220	15
A-21	3-contact med	50/150/DPK	120	3-Way—pink	1,500	...	...
A-23	3-contact med	50/250	120	3-Way—white	1,500	4,240	17
A-19	Med	60A/W	120	White	1,000	855	14
A-19	Med	60A/D	120	Daylight	1,000	500	8
A-19	Med	60A/SB	120	Silvered bowl	1,000	740	12
A-19	Med	60A/Y	120	Yellow bug-light	1,000	550	9
A-19	Med	60A/DPK	120	Pink	1,000	...	...
B-10	Cand	60BC	120	Clear—decorative	1,500	...	...
CA-9	Med	60CAM	120	Clear—bent tip	1,500	...	...
CA-10	Cand	60CAC	120	Clear—bent tip	1,500	...	...
G-40	Med	60G40/W	120	White—decorative	2,500	...	...
G-40	Med	60G40	120	Clear—decorative	2,500	...	...
A-21	Med	60A21/B	120	Blue	1,000	...	...
A-21	Med	60A21/G	120	Green	1,000	...	...
A-21	Med	60A21/0	120	Orange	1,000	...	...
A-21	Med	60A21/R	120	Red	1,000	...	...
A-21	Med	60A21/Y	120	Yellow	1,000	...	...
A-21	Med	67A21/TS	120	Clear—traffic signal	8,000	635	9
A-19	Med	75A/W	120	White	750	1,170	16
A-19	Med	75A/DPK	120	Pink	1,000	...	...
PAR-38	Med	75PAR/FL	120	PAR—flood	2,000	765	10
PAR-38	Med	75PAR/SP	120	PAR—spot	2,000	765	10
PAR-38	Med side prong	75PAR/3FL	120	PAR—compact flood	2,000	765	10
PAR-38	Med side prong	75PAR/3FL	120	PAR—compact flood	2,000	765	10
R-30	Med	75R30/FL	120	Reflector—flood	2,000	900	12
R-30	Med	75R30/SP	120	Reflector—spot	2,000	900	12
R-30	Med	75R30/A	120	Reflector—amber	2,000	...	...
R-30	Med	75R30/B	120	Reflector—blue	2,000	...	...
R-30	Med	75R30/BW	120	Reflector—blue-white	2,000	...	...
R-30	Med	75R30/G	120	Reflector—green	2,000	...	...
R-30	Med	75R30/PK	120	Reflector—pink	2,000	...	...
R-30	Med	75R30/R	120	Reflector—red	2,000	...	...
R-30	Med	75R30/Y	120	Reflector—yellow	2,000	...	...
ER-30	Med	75ER30	120	Elliptical reflector	2,000	850	11

TABLE A.1. (*Continued*)   Incandescent lamps

Bulb size	Base	Ordering abbreviation	Volts	Description	Life (hours)	Initial lumens	Lumens per watt
PAR-38	Med	90PAR/FL/H	120	Halogen flood	2,000	1,270	14
PAR-38	Med	90PAR/SP/H	120	Halogen spot	2,000	1,270	14
PAR-38	Med	90PAR/NSP/H	120	Halogen narrow spot	2,000	1,270	14
A-19	Med	100A/W	120	White	750	1,710	17
A-21	Med	100A21/SB	120	Silvered bowl	1,000	. . .	. . .
A-19	Med	100A/Y	120	Yellow bug light	1,000	1,010	10
A-19	Med	100A/DPK	120	Pink	1,000	. . .	. . .
G-40	Med	100G40/W	120	White – decorative	2,500	1,110	12
G-40	Med	100G40	120	Clear – decorative	2,500	1,230	13
A-23	Med	100A/B	120	Blue	750	. . .	. . .
A-23	Med	100A/G	120	Green	750	. . .	. . .
A-23	Med	100A/O	120	Orange	750	. . .	. . .
A-23	Med	100A/R	120	Red	750	. . .	. . .
A-21	Med	100A21/TS	120	Clear – traffic signal	3,000	1,280	13
G16½	SC bay	100G16/½ 29SC	120	Clear – spot	200	1,660	17
G16½	DC bay	100G16½/ 29DC	120	Clear – spot	200	1,660	17
PAR-38	Med	100PAR/FL	120	PAR – flood	2,000	1,200	12
PAR-38	Med	100PAR/SP	120	PAR – spot	2,000	1,200	12
PAR-38	Med	100PAR/A	120	PAR – amber	2,000	. . .	. . .
PAR-38	Med	100PAR/B	120	PAR – blue	2,000	. . .	. . .
PAR-38	Med	100PAR/BW	120	PAR – blue-white	2,000	. . .	. . .
PAR-38	Med	100PAR/G	120	PAR – green	2,000	. . .	. . .
PAR-38	Med	100PAR/PK	120	PAR – pink	2,000	. . .	. . .
PAR-38	Med	100PAR/R	120	PAR – red	2,000	. . .	. . .
PAR-38	Med	100PAR/Y	120	PAR – yellow	2,000	. . .	. . .
R-40	Med	100R/FL	120	Reflector – flood	2,000	. . .	. . .
R-40	Med	100R/SP	120	Reflector – spot	2,000	. . .	. . .
PS-30	3-contact mogul	100/300	120	3-Way – white	1,500	4,940	16
A-21	Med	116A21/TS	120	Clear – traffic signal	8,000	1,280	11
PAR-56	Screw	120PAR56/VNSP	12	PAR – very narrow spot	2,000	. . .	. . .
PAR-56	Screw	120PAR56/MFL	12	PAR – medium flood	2,000	. . .	. . .
PAR-56	Screw	120PAR56/WF	12	PAR – wide flood	2,000	. . .	. . .
A-21	Med	150A/W	120	White	750	2,780	19
PS-25	Med	150PS25/Y	120	Yellow bug light	1,000	1,560	10
PS-25	Med	150/SB	120	Silvered bowl	1,000	2,370	16
PAR-38	Med	150PAR/FL	120	PAR – flood	2,000	1,740	12
PAR-38	Med	150PAR/WFL	120	PAR – wide flood	2,000	1,740	12
PAR-38	Med side prong	150PAR/3FL	120	PAR – compact flood	2,000	1,740	12
PAR-38	Med	150PAR/SP	120	PAR – spot	2,000	1,740	12
PAR-38	Med side prong	150PAR/3SP	120	PAR – compact spot	2,000	1,740	12
PAR-38	Med	150PAR/FL/A	120	PAR – amber	2,000	. . .	. . .
PAR-38	Med	150PAR/FL/B	120	PAR – blue	2,000	. . .	. . .
PAR-38	Med	150PAR/FL/G	120	PAR – green	2,000	. . .	. . .
PAR-38	Med	150PAR/FL/R	120	PAR – red	2,000	. . .	. . .
PAR-38	Med	150PAR/FL/Y	120	PAR – yellow	2,000	. . .	. . .
R-40	Med	150R/FL	120	Reflector – flood	2,000	1,900	13
R-40	Med	150R/SP	120	Reflector – spot	2,000	1,900	13
R-40	Med	150R/A	120	Reflector – amber	2,000	. . .	. . .
R-40	Med	150R/B	120	Reflector – blue	2,000	. . .	. . .
R-40	Med	150R/BW	120	Reflector – blue-white	2,000	. . .	. . .
R-40	Med	150R/G	120	Reflector – green	2,000	. . .	. . .
R-40	Med	150R/PK	120	Reflector – pink	2,000	. . .	. . .

TABLE A.1. (*Continued*)   Incandescent lamps

Bulb size	Base	Ordering abbreviation	Volts	Description	Life (hours)	Initial lumens	Lumens per watt
R-40	Med	150R/R	120	Reflector—red	2,000	...	...
R-40	Med	150R/Y	120	Reflector—yellow	2,000	...	...
R-40	Med	150R/TB	120	Reflector—transparent blue	2,000	...	...
A-21	Med	200/W	120	White	750	3,910	20
PS-30	Med	200/SBIF	120	Silvered bowl	1,000	3,320	17
PAR-46	Med side prong	200PAR/3NSP	120	PAR—narrow spot	2,000	2,300	12
PAR-46	Med side prong	200/PAR/3MFL	120	PAR—medium flood	2,000	2,300	12
PAR-56	Screw	240PAR56VNSP	12	PAR—very narrow spot	2,000	...	...
PAR-56	Screw	240PAR56MF	12	PAR—medium flood	2,000	...	...
PAR-56	Screw	240PAR56WFL	12	PAR—wide flood	2,000	...	...
R-40	Med	250R40/1	120	Reflector—infrared, heat	5,000+	...	...
R-40	Med	250R40/10	120	Reflector—infrared, red end	5,000+	...	...
PS-25	Med	300M/IF	120	Inside frost	750	6,360	21
PS-35	Med	300MS/SBIF	120	Silver bowl	1,000	...	...
PS-35	Mogul	300/IF	120	Inside frost	1,000	5,820	19
PS-35	Mogul	300/SBIF	120	Silver bowl	1,000	5,410	18
PAR-56	Mogul end prong	300PAR56/NSP	120	PAR—narrow spot	2,000	3,840	13
PAR-56	Mogul end prong	300PAR56/MFL	120	PAR—medium flood	2,000	3,840	13
PAR-56	Mogul end prong	300PAR56/WFL	120	PAR—wide flood	2,000	3,840	13
R-40	Med	300R/FL	120	Reflector—flood	2,000	3,650	12
R-40	Mogul	300R/3FL	120	Reflector—flood	2,000	3,650	12
R-40	Med	300R/SP	120	Reflector—spot	2,000	3,650	12
R-40	Mogul	300R/3SP	120	Reflector—spot	2,000	3,650	12
PS-35	Mogul	500/IF	120	Inside frost	1,000	10,850	22
PAR-64	Mogul end prong	500PAR64/NSP	120	PAR—narrow spot	2,000	6,500	13
PAR-64	Mogul end prong	500PAR64/MFL	120	PAR—medium flood	2,000	6,500	13
PAR-64	Mogul end prong	500PAR64/WFL	120	PAR—wide flood	2,000	6,500	13
R-40	Mogul	500R/3FL	120	Reflector—flood	2,000	6,500	13
R-40	Mogul	500R/3SP	120	Reflector—spot	2,000	6,500	13
R-52	Mogul	500R52	120	Reflector	2,000	7,600	15
PS-52	Mogul	750/IF	120	Inside frost	1,000	17,040	23
PS-52	Mogul	750/SBIF	120	IF—silver bowl	1,000	...	...
R-52	Mogul	750R52	120	Reflector	2,000	13,000	17
PS-52	Mogul	1000/IF	120	Inside frost	1,000	23,740	24
PS-52	Mogul	1000/SBIF	120	IF—silver bowl	1,000	20,400	20
R-52	Mogul	1M/R52	120	Reflector	2,000	...	...
PS-52	Mogul	1500	120	Clear	1,000	34,400	23

TABLE A.2. Quartz lamps

Bulb size	Base	Ordering abbreviation	Volts	Description	Life (hours)	Initial lumens	Lumens per watt
MR-16	2-Pin	Q20MR16/NSP	12	Narrow spot — 13°	3,000	260	13
MR-16	2-Pin	Q20MR16/VNSP	12	V. narrow spot — 7°	3,000	255	13
MR-16	2-Pin	Q20MR16/FL	12	Flood — 40°	3,000	260	13
MR-16	2-Pin	Q42MR16/VNSP	12	V. narrow spot — 9°	3,500	630	15
MR-16	2-Pin	Q42MR16/NFL	12	Narrow flood — 27°	3,000	630	15
MR-16	2-Pin	Q50MR16/NSP	12	Narrow spot — 14°	3,000	895	18
MR-16	2-Pin	Q50MR16/NFL	12	Narrow flood — 27°	3,000	895	18
MR-16	2-Pin	Q50MR16/FL	12	Flood — 40°	3,000	895	18
MR-16	2-Pin	Q75MR16/NSP	12	Narrow spot — 14°	3,500	1,300	17
MR-16	2-Pin	Q75MR16/FL	12	Flood — 42°	3,500	1,300	17
MR-16	2-Pin	Q75MR16/NFL	12	Narrow flood — 25°	3,500	1,300	17
T-4	Minican	Q100CL/MC	120	Clear	1,000	1,800	18
T-4	DC bay	Q100CL/DC	120	Clear	1,000	1,800	18
T-4	Minican	Q150CL/MC	120	Clear	2,000	2,800	19
T-4	DC bay	Q150CL/DC	120	Clear	2,000	2,800	19
PAR-38	Med	Q150PAR38/SP	120	PAR — spot	4,000	2,000	13
PAR-38	Med	Q150PAR38/FL	120	PAR — flood	4,000	2,000	13
T-3	Rec SC	Q200T3/CL	120	Clear	1,500	3,460	17
PAR-38	Med	Q250PAR38/SP	120	PAR — spot	6,000	3,500	14
PAR-38	Med	Q250PAR38/FL	120	PAR — flood	6,000	3,500	14
T-4	Minican	Q250CL/MC	120	Clear	2,000	5,000	20
T-4	DC bay	Q250CL/DC	120	Clear	2,000	5,000	20
T-3	Rec SC	Q300T3/CL	120	Clear	2,000	5,950	20
T-4	Rec SC	Q400T4/CL	120	Clear	2,000	7,750	19
T-4	Minican	Q400CL/MC	120	Clear	2,000	8,250	21
T-3	Rec SC	Q500T3/CL	120	Clear	2,000	11,100	22
T-4	DC bay	Q500CL/DC	120	Clear	2,000	10,450	21
PAR-56	Mogul end prong	Q500PAR56/NSP	120	PAR — narrow spot	4,000	8,000	16
PAR-56	Mogul end prong	Q500PAR56/MFL	120	PAR — medium flood	4,000	8,000	16
PAR-56	Mogul end prong	Q500PAR56/WFL	120	PAR — wide flood	4,000	8,000	16
T-3	Rec SC	Q1000T3/CL	240	Clear	2,000	21,500	21
PAR-64	Mogul end prong	Q1000PAR64/NSP	120	PAR — narrow spot	4,000	19,400	19
PAR-64	Mogul end prong	Q1000PAR64/MFL	120	PAR — medium flood	4,000	19,400	19
PAR-64	Mogul end prong	Q1000PAR64/WFL	120	PAR — wide flood	4,000	19,400	19
R-60	Mogul	Q1000R60FL	120	Reflector — flood	3,000	18,300	18
T-3	Rec SC	Q1500T3/CL	208/277	Clear	2,000	35,800	24

Note: DC bay = double-contact bayonet, Rec SC = recessed single contact.

TABLE A.3.   Mercury lamps

Bulb shape	Base	Ordering abbreviation	Description	Apparent color temperature/ color rendition	Life (hours)	Initial lumens	Lumens per watt
E-17	Med	H75DX43	Deluxe white	3900/50	16,000	2,800	37
E-23½	Mogul	H100DX38	Deluxe white	3900/50	24,000	4,200	42
E-23½	Mogul	H100WDX38	Warm deluxe	3300/50	24,000	3,400	34
R-40	Med	H100RFL38	Reflector – clear	5710/15	24,000	2,850	28
E-28	Mogul	H175DX39	Deluxe white	3900/50	24,000	8,600	49
E-28	Mogul	H175WDX39	Warm deluxe	3300/50	24,000	7,000	40
R-40	Med	H175RFL39	Reflector – clear	5710/15	24,000	5,700	32
E-28	Mogul	H250DX37	Deluxe white	3900/50	24,000	12,100	48
E-28	Mogul	H250WDX37	Warm deluxe	3300/50	24,000	10,000	40
E-37	Mogul	H400DX33	Deluxe white	3900/50	24,000	22,500	56
E-37	Mogul	H400WDX33	Warm deluxe	3300/50	24,000	19,500	49
BT-56	Mogul	H1000DX36	Deluxe white	3900/50	24,000	63,000	63

Note: Med = medium.

TABLE A.4.   Metal halide lamps (metalarc, multivapor)

Bulb shape	Base	Ordering abbreviation	Description	Apparent color temperature/ color rendition	Life (hours)	Initial lumens	Lumens per watt
E-17	Med	MX32/C	Clear – special position	3000/65	7,500	2,500	78
E-28	Mogul	MV175	Clear	4100/65	10,000	14,000	80
E-28	Mogul	MV175/C	Phosphored	3900/70	10,000	14,000	80
E-23½	Mogul	MX175/3K	Clear	3000/65	10,000	16,600	95
E-23½	Mogul	MX175/C3K	Phosphored	3000/65	10,000	15,750	90
E-28	Mogul	MV250	Clear	4100/65	10,000	20,500	82
E-28	Mogul	MV250/C	Phosphored	3900/70	10,000	20,500	82
E-37	Mogul	MV400	Clear	4000/65	20,000	36,000	90
E-37	Mogul	MV400/C	Phosphored	3700/70	20,000	36,000	90
E-37	Mogul	MV400	Clear – special position	4000/65	20,000	40,000	100
E-37	Mogul	MV400/C	Phosphored – special position	3700/70	20,000	40,000	100
BT-56	Mogul	MV1000	Clear	3800/65	12,000	110,000	110
BT-56	Mogul	MV1000/C	Phosphored	3400/70	12,000	105,000	105

TABLE A.5.   High-pressure sodium lamps (lucalox, ceramalux, unalux)

Bulb shape	Base	Ordering abbreviation	Description	Apparent color temperature/ color rendition	Life (hours)	Initial lumens	Lumens per watt
E-17	Med	LU35/MED	Clear & diffuse	1900/21	20,000	2,250	64
R-38	Med	LU35/RFL	Flood	1900/20	16,000	1,400	40
E-17	Med	LU50/MED	Clear & diffuse	1900/21	24,000	4,000	80
E-23½	Mogul	LU50	Clear & diffuse	1900/21	24,000	4,000	80
E-17	Med	LU70/MED	Clear & diffuse	1900/21	24,000	5,800	83
E-23½	Mogul	LU70	Clear & diffuse	1900/21	24,000	5,800	83
R-38	Med	LU70/RFL	Flood	1900/20	16,000	3,400	49
E-17	Med	LU70/DX/MED	Improved color	2200/65	10,000	3,800	54
E-17	Med	LU100/MED	Clear & diffuse	2100/21	24,000	9,500	95
E-23½	Mogul	LU100	Clear & diffuse	2100/21	24,000	9,500	95
E-17	Med	LU150/MED	Clear & diffuse	2100/21	24,000	16,000	107
E-23½	Mogul	LU150	Clear & diffuse	2100/21	24,000	16,000	107
E-18	Mogul	LU200	Clear	2100/21	24,000	22,000	110
E-18	Mogul	LU250	Clear & diffuse	2100/21	24,000	27,500	110
E-18	Mogul	LU250/DX	Improved color	2200/65	10,000	22,500	90
E-18	Mogul	LU400	Clear & diffuse	2100/21	24,000	50,000	125
E-25	Mogul	LU1000	Clear	2100/21	24,000	140,000	140

TABLE A.6. Fluorescent lamps

Lamp watts	Bulb	Length, including sockets (inches)	Ordering abbreviation	Description	Apparent color temperature/ color rendition	Life (hours)	Initial lumens	Lumens per watt
4	T-5	6	F4T5/CW	Cool white	4150/62	6,000	135	34
4	T-5	6	F4T5/BL	Black light	. . .	6,000	. . .	. . .
4	T-5	6	F4T5/BLB	BL blue	. . .	6,000	. . .	. . .
6	T-5	9	F6T5/CW	Cool white	4150/62	7,500	295	49
6	T-5	9	F6T5/CWX	CW deluxe	4175/89	7,500	205	34
6	T-5	9	F6T5/BLB	BL blue	. . .	7,500	. . .	. . .
8	T-5	12	F8T5/CW	Cool white	4150/62	7,500	400	50
8	T-5	12	F8T5/CWX	CW deluxe	4175/89	7,500	275	34
8	T-5	12	F8T5/WW	Warm white	3000/52	7,500	385	48
8	T-5	12	F8T5/BLB	BL blue	. . .	7,500	. . .	. . .
13	T-5	21	F13T5/CW	Cool white	4150/62	7,500	820	63
13	T-8	12	F13T8/CW	Cool white	4150/62	7,500	500	38
14	T-8	15	F14T8/CW	Cool white	4150/62	7,500	650	46
14	T-12	15	F14T12/CW	Cool white	4150/62	9,000	675	48
14	T-12	15	F14T12/WWX	WW deluxe	3025/77	9,000	460	33
15	T-8	18	F15T8/CW	Cool white	4150/62	7,500	870	58
15	T-8	18	F15T8/WWX	WW deluxe	3025/77	7,500	505	34
15	T-8	18	F15T8/CWX	CW deluxe	4175/89	7,500	610	41
15	T-8	18	F15T8/WW	Warm white	3000/52	7,500	870	58
15	T-8	18	F15T8/PL	Plant light	6750/31	7,500	250	17
15	T-8	18	F15T8/R	Red	. . .	7,500	40	3
15	T-8	18	F15T8/BL	Black light	. . .	7,500	. . .	. . .
15	T-8	18	F15T8/BLB	BL blue	. . .	7,500	. . .	. . .
15	T-12	18	F15T12/CW	Cool white	4150/62	9,000	800	53
15	T-12	18	F15T12/WWX	WW deluxe	3025/77	9,000	505	34
15	T-12	18	F15T12/WW	Warm white	3000/52	9,000	800	53
20	T-12	24	F20T12/CW	Cool white	4150/62	9,000	1,250	62
20	T-12	24	F20T12/SP35	3500 K	3500/73	9,000	1,290	64
20	T-12	24	F20T12/SP30	3000 K	3000/70	9,000	1,340	67
20	T-12	24	F20T12/WWX	WW deluxe	3025/77	9,000	820	41
20	T-12	24	F20T12/CWX	CW deluxe	4175/89	9,000	850	42
20	T-12	24	F20T12/WW	Warm white	3000/52	9,000	1,300	65
20	T-12	24	F20T12/C50	Chroma 50	5000/90	9,000	850	42
20	T-12	24	F20T12/PL	Plant light	6750/31	9,000	340	17
20	T-12	24	F20T12/B	Blue	. . .	9,000	450	22
20	T-12	24	F20T12/G	Green	6975/. .	9,000	1,650	82
20	T-12	24	F20T12/GO	Gold	2500/38	9,000	900	45
20	T-12	24	F20T12/PK	Pink	. . .	9,000	450	22
20	T-12	24	F20T12/BL	Black light	. . .	9,000	. . .	. . .
20	T-12	24	F20T12/BLB	BL blue	. . .	9,000	. . .	. . .
30	T-8	36	F30T8/CW	Cool white	4150/62	7,500	2,300	73
30	T-8	36	F30T8/WWX	WW deluxe	3025/77	7,500	1,400	47
30	T-8	36	F30T8/CWX	CW deluxe	4175/89	7,500	1,500	50
30	T-8	36	F30T8/WW	Warm white	3000/52	7,500	2,300	77
30	T-8	36	F30T8/PL	Plant light	6750/31	7,500	600	20
30	T-12	36	F30T12/CW	Cool white	4150/62	18,000	2,300	77
30	T-12	36	F30T12/SP35	3500 K	3500/73	18,000	2,270	76
30	T-12	36	F30T12/SPX30	3000 K	3000/82	18,000	2,400	80
30	T-12	36	F30T12/CWX	CW deluxe	4175/89	18,000	1,530	51
30	T-12	36	F30T12/WWX	WW deluxe	3025/77	18,000	1,490	50
30	T-12	36	F30T12/WW	Warm white	3000/52	18,000	2,360	79
30	T-12	36	F30T12/C50	5000 K	5000/90	18,000	1,600	53

Note: Not all available colors are shown for each size.
BL = black light, CW = cool white, WW = warm white, K = degrees Kelvin.

TABLE A.6. (Continued)   Fluorescent lamps

Lamp watts	Bulb	Length, including sockets (inches)	Ordering abbreviation	Description	Apparent color temperature/ color rendition	Life (hours)	Initial lumens	Lumens per watt
40	T-12	48	F40CW	Cool white	4150/62	20,000	3,150	79
40	T-12	48	F40SP41	4100 K	4100/70	20,000	3,240	81
40	T-12	48	F40SP35	3500 K	3500/73	20,000	3,180	80
40	T-12	48	48F40SPX35	3500K	3500/82	20,000	3,210	80
40	T-12	48	F40SP30	3000 K	3000/70	20,000	3,230	81
40	T-12	48	F40SPX30	3000K	3000/82	20,000	3,250	81
40	T-12	48	F40CWX	CW deluxe	4175/89	20,000	2,500	56
40	T-12	48	F40WWX	WW deluxe	3025/77	20,000	2,200	55
40	T-12	48	F40WW	Warm white	3000/52	20,000	3,200	80
40	T-12	48	F40C50	5000 K	5000/90	20,000	2,200	55
40	T-12	48	F40IF	Incandescent/ fluorescent	2750/89	20,000	1,720	43
40	T-12	48	F40PL	Plant light	6750/31	20,000	850	21
40	T-12	48	F40B	Blue	...	20,000	1,200	30
40	T-12	48	F40G	Green	6975/..	20,000	4,350	109
40	T-12	48	F40GO	Gold	2500/38	20,000	2,400	60
40	T-12	48	F40PK	Pink	...	20,000	1,100	28
40	T-12	48	F40R	Red	...	20,000	200	5
40	T-12	48	F40BL	Black light	...	20,000	...	...
40	T-12	48	F40BLB	BL blue	...	20,000	...	...

TABLE A.7.   Energy-saving lamps

Lamp watts	Bulb	Length, including sockets (inches)	Ordering abbreviation	Description	Apparent color temperature/ color rendition	Life (hours)	Initial lumens	Lumens per watt
34	T-12	48	F40CW/RS/WM	Cool white	4150/62	20,000	2,750	81
34	T-12	48	F40SP41/RS/WM	4100 K	4100/70	20,000	2,850	84
34	T-12	48	F40SP35/RS/WM	3500 K	3500/73	20,000	2,900	85
34	T-12	48	F40SPX35/RS/WM	3500K	3500/82	20,000	2,850	84
34	T-12	48	F40SP30/RS/WM	3000 K	3000/70	20,000	2,900	85
34	T-12	48	F40SPX30/RS/WM	3000/K	3000/82	20,000	2,850	84
34	T-12	48	F40CWX/RS/WM	CW deluxe	4175/89	20,000	1,925	57
34	T-12	48	F40WWX/RS/WM	WW deluxe	3025/79	20,000	1,925	57
34	T-12	48	F40WW/RS/WM	Warm white	3000/52	20,000	2,800	82
34	T-12	48	F40LW/RS/WM	Lite white	4200/49	20,000	2,925	86

Note: CW = cool white, WW = warm white, K = degrees Kelvin.

TABLE A.8.   Higher-light-output lamps

Lamp watts	Bulb	Length, including sockets (inches)	Ordering abbreviation	Description	Apparent color temperature/ color rendition	Life (hours)	Initial lumens	Lumens per watt
40	T-12	48	F40LW/MM	Lite white	4200/49	15,000	3,450	86
40	T-12	48	F40SP41/MM	4100 K	4100/70	15,000	3,350	84
40	T-12	48	F40SP35/MM	3500 K	3500/73	15,000	3,350	84
40	T-12	48	F40SP30/MM	3000 K	3000/70	15,000	3,350	84

Note: K = degrees Kelvin.

TABLE A.9. U-shaped lamps

Lamp watts	Bulb	Length, including sockets (inches)	Ordering abbreviation	Description	Apparent color temperature/ color rendition	Life (hours)	Initial lumens	Lumens per watt
40	T-12	24	F40CW/U3	Cool white	4150/62	12,000	2,825	71
40	T-12	24	F40SP35/U3	3500 K	3500/73	12,000	2,935	73
40	T-12	24	F40CWX/U3	CW deluxe	4175/89	12,000	2,020	50
40	T-12	24	F40WWX/U3	WW deluxe	3025/77	12,000	1,850	46
40	T-12	24	F40WW/U3	Warm white	3000/52	12,000	2,925	73

Note: All lamps are available in 6-inch leg spacing.
CW = cool white, WW = warm white, K = degrees Kelvin.

TABLE A.10. Circline lamps

Lamp watts	Bulb	Diameter (inches)	Ordering abbreviation	Description	Apparent color temperature/ color rendition	Life (hours)	Initial lumens	Lumens per watt
20	T-9	6½	FC6T9/CW	Cool white	4150/62	12,000	800	40
22	T-9	8¼	FC8T9/CW	Cool white	4150/62	12,000	1,050	48
32	T-9	12	FC12T9/CW	Cool white	4150/62	12,000	1,900	59
40	T-9	16	FC16T9/CW	Cool white	4150/62	12,000	2,600	65

TABLE A.11. Slimline lamps (single pin–instant start)

Lamp watts	Bulb	Length, including sockets (inches)	Ordering abbreviation	Description	Apparent color temperature/ color rendition	Life (hours)	Initial lumens	Lumens per watt
20	T-12	24	F24T12/CW	Cool white	4150/62	7,500	1,150	58
30	T-12	36	F36T12/CW	Cool white	4150/62	7,500	2,000	67
25	T-6	42	F42T6/CW	Cool white	4150/62	7,500	1,750	70
35	T-12	42	F42T12/CW	Cool white	4150/62	7,500	2,070	59
40	T-12	48	F48T12/CW	Cool white	4150/62	9,000	3,000	75
50	T-12	60	F60T12/CW	Cool white	4150/62	12,000	3,550	71
40	T-6	64	F64T6/CW	Cool white	4150/62	7,500	2,800	70
50	T-12	64	F64T12/CW	Cool white	4150/62	12,000	3,850	77
35	T-8	72	F72T8/CW	Cool white	4150/62	7,500	3,000	86
55	T-12	72	F72T12/CW	Cool white	4150/62	12,000	4,700	85
65	T-12	84	F84T12/CW	Cool white	4150/62	12,000	5,400	83
50	T-8	96	F96T8/CW	Cool white	4150/62	7,500	4,200	84
75	T-12	96	F96T12/CW	Cool white	4150/62	12,000	6,300	84
60	T-12	96	F96T12/LW	Lite white	4200/49	12,000	6,000	100

TABLE A.12. High-output lamps

Lamp watts	Bulb	Length, including sockets (inches)	Ordering abbreviation	Description	Apparent color temperature/ color rendition	Life (hours)	Initial lumens	Lumens per watt
25	T-12	18	F18T12/CW/HO	Cool white	4150/62	9,000	1,060	42
35	T-12	24	F24T12/CW/HO	Cool white	4150/62	9,000	1,700	49
45	T-12	36	F36T12/CW/HO	Cool white	4150/62	9,000	2,850	63
55	T-12	42	F42T12/CW/HO	Cool white	4150/62	9,000	3,500	64
60	T-12	48	F48T12/CW/HO	Cool white	4150/62	12,000	4,300	72
85	T-12	72	F72T12/CW/HO	Cool white	4150/62	12,000	6,650	78
110	T-12	96	F96T12/CW/HO	Cool white	4150/62	12,000	9,200	84
95	T-12	96	F96T12/LW/HO	Lite white	4200/49	12,000	8,800	93

TABLE A.13. 1500-milliampere lamps (power groove, SHO, VHO)

Lamp watts	Bulb	Length, including sockets (inches)	Ordering abbreviation	Description	Apparent color temperature/ color rendition	Life (hours)	Initial lumens	Lumens per watt
110	PG-17	48	F48PG17/CW	Cool white	4150/62	12,000	6,900	63
165	PG-17	72	F72PG17/CW	Cool white	4150/62	12,000	11,500	70
215	PG-17	96	F96PG17/CW	Cool white	4150/62	12,000	16,000	74
185	PG-17	96	F96PG17/LW	Lite white	4200/49	12,000	14,900	81
110	T-12	48	F48T12/1500/CW	Cool white	4150/62	10,000	6,500	59
165	T-12	72	F72T12/1500/CW	Cool white	4150/62	10,000	10,000	61
215	T-12	96	F96T12/1500/CW	Cool white	4150/62	10,000	14,000	65
185	T-12	96	F96T12/LW	Lite white	4200/49	9,000	13,800	75

Note: SHO = super high output, VHO = very high output.

GLOSSARY

AMBIENT LIGHTING — Lighting system used to supply general as opposed to task lighting in a space. Walking-around light.

ANGSTROM — Used to designate wavelengths; 0.0000000001 meters.

APPARENT COLOR TEMPERATURE — Temperature, in degrees Kelvin, of a theoretical black body (material that reflects no light) having the same color appearance as the source being viewed. The higher the number, the bluer the source.

BALLAST — Used with discharge lamps to limit current and provide proper electrical values to the lamp.

BLACK BODY — Absorbs all light hitting it. Used in connection with color temperature of sources.

BLACK LIGHT — Near ultraviolet (320 to 400 nanometers). Not really light at all. Used to produce showy effects and to attract insects.

BRACKET — Wall-mounted lighting fixture consisting of a shielding board in front of a fluorescent strip.

BULB — Glass part of a light bulb.

CANDLE (CANDLEPOWER, CANDELA) — Unit of brightness. Used with relatively high values such as those for fixtures and lamps.

CANDLEPOWER (cp) CURVE — Photometric curve showing brightnesses of a fixture or lamp at various viewing angles. Used in calculating coefficients of utilization.

CATHODE — Used in discharge lamps to conduct electricity in and out of the arc.

CATHODE RAY TUBE (CRT) — Video, TV, computer.

CAVITY RATIO — Ratio of the wall area to that of the horizontal area of the room, ceiling, or floor cavity.

CEILING CAVITY RATIO — Ratio of the wall area above the lighting fixtures to the ceiling area. Used in determining coefficients of utilization.

CERTIFIED BALLAST MANUFACTURERS (CBM) — Industry organization that certifies performance of approved ballasts.

CHANNEL — Enclosure housing the wiring, ballast(s), starters, and lamp-holders for one or more fluorescent lamps.

COEFFICIENT OF UTILIZATION (CU) — Percentage of lumens emitted by the lamp that eventually reaches the work plane. Used in zonal cavity illumination calculations.

COLOR RENDERING INDEX (CRI) — Scale of values from 0 to 100, indicating how a light source makes colors look compared to a reference source of the same color temperature. Not a perfect measurement, but the best we have.

COLOR RENDITION — The ability of a light source to make pigments look like the viewer thinks they should.

COLOR TEMPERATURE — Blueness or redness of a light source. Often incorrectly used in place of *apparent color temperature* or *correlated color temperature.*

CONTRAST — Brightness difference between surfaces in the field of view.

CORNICE — Structural lighting element that casts light downward only. Usually fluorescent.

CORRELATED COLOR TEMPERATURE — Temperature, in degrees Kelvin, of a theoretical black body (material that reflects no light) having the same color appearance as the source being viewed. The higher the number, the bluer the source.

COVE — Structural lighting element that casts light upward only. Upside-down cornice.

CRI — Color rendering index.

CRT — Cathode ray tube. Video. TV. Computer.

CU — Coefficient of utilization.

DIFFUSED LIGHTING — Light arriving at a point from many directions.

DIFFUSER — Light control media that is uniformly bright at all viewing angles.

DIRECT GLARE — Visual discomfort due to excessive brightness of a light source.

DIRECT LIGHTING — Lighting system that emits at least 90 percent of its output toward the floor.

DISCHARGE LAMP — Lamp producing light by means of an arc through a gas.

DOWNLIGHT — Open-bottomed fixture normally containing an incandescent or high-intensity discharge lamp. Usually casts little light on vertical surfaces.

EFFICACY — Engineering term meaning efficiency of light production per power input. Lumens per watt.

EFFICIENCY — Common term for lumens per watt. Amount of light out for amount of power in.

ELECTRICAL TESTING LABORATORIES (ETL) — Perform safety and performance evaluations.

ELECTRIC DISCHARGE LAMP — Lamp that produces light by means of electric current flowing through a gas. Includes fluorescent and high-intensity discharge lamps.

ELECTROMAGNETIC SPECTRUM — The entire range of radiant energy propagated by waves. Includes light, ultraviolet, infrared, etc.

EMISSION MIX — Chemical powder that aids in discharge lamp operation.

EQUIVALENT SPHERE ILLUMINATION (ESI) — Light level from a theoretically perfect lighting system equaling the same visibility as the real system.

ERYTHEMAL ULTRAVIOLET — Radiation that produces reddening of the skin. About 297 nanometers.

ESI — Equivalent sphere illumination.

ETL — Electrical Testing Laboratories.

EYE SENSITIVITY CURVE — Shows response of the eye to various wavelengths of light.

FAR ULTRAVIOLET — From about 180 to 280 nanometers.

FILAMENT — Wire inside an incandescent lamp that produces light when heated by electric current. Usually made of tungsten.

FIXTURE — Common name for a luminaire containing one or more lamps and associated sockets, reflectors, lenses, etc.

FLOOR CAVITY RATIO — Ratio of wall area below the work plane to floor area. Used in determining coefficients of utilization.

FLOOR LAMP — Portable fixture resting on the floor.

FLUORESCENT LAMP — Discharge lamp that produces light by means of electric current through low-pressure mercury gas. The arc produces ultraviolet energy that is converted into light by a phosphor coating on the glass bulb.

FOOTCANDLE (fc) — One lumen per square foot. Used in designating lighting levels and determining brightnesses.

FOOTLAMBERT (fL) — Brightness of a surface reflecting or emitting one lumen per square foot. A reflected footcandle. Used to designate relatively low brightnesses such as room surfaces.

FREQUENCY — In the electromagnetic spectrum, measures the number of times per second an energy wave passes a given point.

GENERAL LIGHTING — System providing approximately even illumination throughout an area.

GERMICIDAL ULTRAVIOLET — Radiation that kills bacteria. About 253 nanometers.

GLARE — Visual discomfort caused by excessive brightness. Can be direct (from a light source, fixture, lamp, window, etc.) or reflected (from the task or other nearby surface).

HERTZ—Cycles per second. Designation of frequency.

HIGH-INTENSITY DISCHARGE (HID) LAMPS—Family of lamps (including mercury, metal halide, and high-pressure sodium) that produces light directly from an electric arc through a gas. Operate at relatively high gas pressure.

HIGH-PRESSURE SODIUM (HPS) LAMP—Discharge lamp containing mostly sodium as the conducting gas. "High pressure" only in relation to "low pressure."

ILLUMINANCE—Word currently in vogue to mean illumination or light level. Commonly expressed in footcandles.

ILLUMINATING ENGINEERING SOCIETY OF NORTH AMERICA (IESNA)—Organization of people interested in lighting, such as users, specifiers, electricity suppliers, or equipment manufacturers. The prime source of scientific lighting research.

INCANDESCENT—Term applied to lamps that produce light by heating a filament to incandescence with electricity. The "light bulb."

INDIRECT LIGHTING—System that emits 90 percent or more of its light toward the ceiling.

INFRARED—Invisible radiation that heats objects it strikes; 780 to 100,000 nanometers.

INSTANT START—Circuit for fluorescent lamps.

INVERSE SQUARE LAW—Formula stating that illumination varies directly as the brightness in a given direction of a point source and inversely as the square of the distance from that source (footcandles equal candlepower divided by distance squared). Used to calculate light levels at a point.

KELVIN—Temperature scale having zero at −273 degrees C. Used in designating the visual appearance of light sources.

KILOWATT—One thousand watts.

KILOWATT-HOUR—One thousand watts used for one hour or one watt used for one thousand hours. The basic billing unit for electric utilities.

LAMP—Manufactured electrical light source.

LAMPHOLDER—Socket.

LAMP LUMEN DEPRECIATION (LLD)—Ratio of mean light output of a lamp throughout its life to its initial rating. Used in footcandle calculations.

LASER—Light amplification by stimulated emission of radiation. Produces a monochromatic (one-color), coherent beam of light. Used for spectacular effects, information transmission, and other purposes.

LDD—Luminaire dirt depreciation.

LENS—Control device formed of glass or plastic used to bend light in desired directions.

LIGHT — Visually evaluated radiant energy. Approximately 380 to 780 nanometers. Stuff you can see by.

LIGHT LOSS FACTOR — Calculation factor used to account for light losses due to dirt, lamp lumen depreciation, and in extremely accurate calculations, temperature, voltage, maintenance practices, and atmospheric conditions.

LLD — Lamp lumen depreciation.

LOUVER — Light control device using concealment of the source to reduce brightness. Sometimes called "eggcrate."

LOW-PRESSURE SODIUM LAMP — Discharge lamp that produces light by passage of current through sodium gas under low pressure. Although highly efficient, it is a very large source and produces only yellow light so that no color discrimination is possible.

LPW — Lumens per watt.

LUMEN (lm) — Amount of light falling on a 1-square-foot surface 1 foot away from a one-candlepower source. Used to indicate output of light sources.

LUMENS PER WATT (LPW) — Yardstick for efficiency of lamps in light production. Light out in return for watts in.

LUMINAIRE — Engineering term for "fixture."

LUMINAIRE DIRT DEPRECIATION (LDD) — Percentage of light lost in a lighting system over time due to dirt on the lamps, fixtures, and room surfaces.

LUMINANCE — Alternate term for brightness. Commonly expressed in footlamberts.

LUMINOUS CEILING — Lighting system using the entire ceiling as a light source.

LUX — International term for light level; 0.0929 footcandles.

MAINTENANCE FACTOR (MF) — Ratio of maintained to initial light levels. Includes *luminaire dirt depreciation* and *lamp lumen depreciation* factors.

MATTE — Not shiny. A blotter has a matte finish.

MERCURY LAMP — High-intensity discharge lamp producing light by passage of electricity through mercury gas. May be phosphor coated for better color rendition.

METAL HALIDE LAMP — High-intensity discharge lamp using mercury and metallic halides in gaseous form. Has higher efficiency and better color rendition than mercury lamps.

METAMERIC COLORS — Two color samples that appear the same under one light source but different under another.

MF — Maintenance factor.

MONOCHROMATIC ENERGY—Energy at only one point in the spectrum.

MORTALITY CURVE—Used to indicate expected burnouts in a group of lamps at various burning hours.

MOUNTING HEIGHT (MH)—Distance from the bottom of the fixture to either the floor or work plane, dependent on usage.

NANOMETER—Unit of length used to designate wavelengths; 0.000000001 meter.

NEAR ULTRAVIOLET—From about 320 to 380 nanometers; "black light."

OZONE—A gas that can be poisonous in sufficient quantities.

PARABOLIC ALUMINIZED REFLECTOR (PAR)—A reflector lamp made of molded hard glass.

PARABOLIC LOUVERS—Louvers whose vertical elements have a parabolic shape. Produce low brightness at normal viewing angles.

POINT-BY-POINT METHOD—Lighting calculation used to determine light levels at particular points in a space. Uses the inverse square law.

POLARIZATION—Light control method that causes light waves to oscillate in only one plane.

PREHEAT—Circuit for fluorescent lamps using a momentary-contact switch or glow-switch starter.

QUARTZ LAMPS—Incandescent lamps with quartz bulbs.

RAPID START—Circuit for fluorescent lamps in which the ballast provides preheating current.

RATED LIFE—Median life of a large group of lamps. Half will burn out before this time and half after.

REFLECTANCE (rf)—Ratio of light leaving a surface to the amount arriving.

REFLECTION FACTOR—Same as reflectance.

REFLECTOR (R) LAMP—Lamp having a reflector built into the blown-glass bulb.

REFRACTION—Light control method whereby light rays are bent by passing through a prism.

RLM FIXTURE—Fluorescent or incandescent fixture featuring a reflector over the lamps.

ROOM CAVITY RATIO (RCR)—Proportions of a space determined from its length, width, and height; $RCR = 5H(L + W)/(L \times W)$.

S/MH—spacing to mounting height.

SOFFIT—Lighting element that casts light downward only. A wide cornice.

SOUND RATING—Method of determining relative noise from a ballast.

SPACING CRITERION (SC)—See *spacing to mounting height ratio.*

SPACING TO MOUNTING HEIGHT (S/MH) RATIO—Ratio of fixture spacing (distance apart) to mounting height above the work plane. Sometimes called *spacing criterion*.

SPECTRUM—Range of electromagnetic radiation.

SPECULAR—Shiny, like a mirror.

STRIP—Simplest fluorescent fixture.

STRUCTURAL FIXTURES—Fixtures appearing to be part of the room structure.

TASK/AMBIENT LIGHTING—One or more lighting systems providing localized light on the seeing task and general lighting in the space.

TASK LIGHTING—Lighting system designed primarily to put light on a seeing task. Usually combined with ambient lighting.

TRACK LIGHTING—Lighting system utilizing fixtures that plug into power strips on the ceiling or wall.

TRANSMITTANCE—Proportion of light that passes through a medium to the amount arriving.

TRIGGER START—Circuit for fluorescent lamps.

TROFFER—Recessed lighting fixture.

ULTRAVIOLET—A portion of the electromagnetic spectrum with wavelengths shorter than light.

UNDERWRITERS LABORATORIES (UL)—Company that performs safety testing.

VALANCE—Structural element that casts light both up and down.

VCP—Visual comfort probability.

VIDEO DISPLAY TERMINAL (VDT)—Usually a computer terminal.

VISUAL COMFORT PROBABILITY (VCP)—A method of forecasting the percentage of people who will be visually comfortable in a specific lighting application.

WATT—When combined with time, electrical power.

WAVELENGTH—Distance between peaks or valleys of energy waves. Angstroms and nanometers are two measurements of length in the electromagnetic spectrum.

WORK PLANE—Imaginary horizontal surface at which a visual task is performed. Assumed to be 30 inches above the floor if not otherwise indicated.

WRAPAROUND—Fluorescent fixture consisting of one or more lamp strips with a plastic diffuser or lens on the bottom and sides.

REFERENCES AND FURTHER READING

Birren, Faber. *Light, Color and Environments*. New York: Van Nostrand Reinhold, 1982.

Cayless, M. A., and A. M. Marsden. *Lamps and Lighting*. Baltimore: Edward Arnold, 1984.

Egan, M. D. *Concepts in Architectural Lighting*. New York: McGraw-Hill, 1983.

Frier, John, and Mary Frier. *Industrial Lighting Systems*. New York: Mc-Graw-Hill, 1980.

General Electric Company, Lighting Business Group. Various application bulletins. Cleveland: General Electric Company.

Gilliatt, Mary, and Douglas Baker. *Lighting Your Home: A Practical Guide*. New York: Pantheon Books, 1979.

Grosslight, Jane. *Light*. Englewood Cliffs, N.J.: Prentice-Hall, 1984.

Helms, Ronald. *Illuminating Engineering for Energy Efficient Luminous Environments*. Englewood Cliffs, N.J.: Prentice-Hall, 1980.

Illuminating Engineering Society of North America. *IES Lighting Handbook*. New York: Illuminating Engineering Society of North America, current edition.

Lam, William M. C. *Perception and Lighting as Formgivers for Architecture*. New York: McGraw-Hill, 1977.

McGraw-Edison Company, Halo Lighting Division. *The Language of Lighting*. Elk Grove Village, Ill.: McGraw-Edison, 1983.

McGuiness, William, Benjamin Stein, and John Reynolds. *Mechanical and Electrical Equipment for Buildings*. New York: Wiley, 1976.

Murdoch, Joseph. *Illuminating Engineering*. New York: Macmillan, 1985.

Nuckolls, James L. *Interior Lighting for Environmental Designers*. New York: Wiley, 1976.

Smith, Fran, and Fred Bertolone. *Bringing Interiors to Light*. Lakewood, N.J.: Whitney, 1986.

PERIODICALS

Architectural Lighting
Interior Design
Lighting Design and Application
Lighting Dimensions
Progressive Architecture
Visual Merchandising and Store Design

INDEX

Absorption, 10, 42, 44
Aluminum, 8
Ambient lighting, 112
Angles, cosines of, 80
Angstrom, 2
Apparent color temperature, 11, 12
Applications, lighting, 92–125
Art galleries, 88
Assembly areas, 88
Audiovisual aids, 122
Auditoriums, 88
Average maintained footcandles, 70–72

Ballasts, 32, 35, 92
  circuits, 33
  electronic, 33
  radio interference, 33
  sound ratings, 32
  temperature ratings, 32
Banks, 88, 123
Bases, lamp, 17, 18, 30
Bathrooms, 88, 99, 102
Beams, 21
Black ceilings, 92
Black light, 2, 3
Book stacks, 122, 125
Brackets, 51, 96, 98, 99, 116
Brightness, 6–8, 86
Bulbs, 18, 35
  shape, 18, 19

Calculations, 61–85
  cavity ratio, 62
  fixture spacing, 73, 74
  lumen method, 70–72
  point-by-point, 79
  sample, 76
Candela, 7
Candle, 7
Candlepower, 7
  curves, 21, 65–69
  formula, 81
Candles per square inch, 7
Cans, 49
Carrels, study, 122
Cases, display, 121
Catalogs

fixture, 65–69
lamp, 126–36
Cathode, 29
Cathode ray tubes (CRT), 90, 114, 122
  screens, 90, 114–16
Cavity ratio, 62–65
  calculating, 62
  table, 63
Ceilings
  black or white, 92, 93
  luminous, 52
  reflectance, 8, 95, 110
  systems, 109, 111
Ceiling cavity ratio, 62
Certified Ballast Manufacturers (CBM), 32
C50, Vitalite, 29
Chandeliers, 49, 104
Channel, wiring, 46
Characteristics, lamp, 39
Circline, 31
Circuit breakers, 54
Circuits, fluorescent, 33
Class P, 32
Classrooms, 88, 121
Clothing displays, 119
Coefficient of utilization (CU), 65, 70, 71
  definition, 65
  source, 71
  tables, 65–69
Coffered ceilings, 111
Color, 2, 10–14
  choice, fluorescent, 29, 40, 41
  expectations, 10
  eye response, 5
  fluorescent, 40
  high-pressure sodium, 38, 39
  mercury, 37, 39
  metal halide, 37, 39
  mixing, 10
  modifying, 10
  primary, 10
  saturation, 14
  secondary, 10
  "white," 12
Color-rendering index (CRI), 12, 40
Color rendition, 12, 39
Color temperature, 11, 12, 40

Commercial lighting, 124
Concealment, 42, 45
Contactor, 54
Contrast, as factor of seeing, 6
Control, lighting, 54–56, 60, 90
  circuit breakers, 54
  dimmers, 55
  low-voltage, 54
  photocells, 55
  switching, 54
  timers, 55
Control, light, 42–45, 90
Cool white, 29
Cool white deluxe, 29
Cornices, 50, 51, 96, 98, 99
Correlated color temperature, 11
Corridors, 88, 124
Cosine table, 80
Cost, light, 57–60
  analysis, 59
  initial, 57
  operating, 58
Coves, 51, 52, 119
Curve, candlepower, 21, 65–69
Curve, mortality, 16
Cycles per second, 2

Daylight, 14, 30, 60, 122
Degrees Kelvin, 11
Depreciation, lamp lumen (LLD), 70
  luminaire dirt (LDD), 70
Design method, 75
  example, 76
Diffusers, 43, 90
Diffusion, 43, 44
Dimmers, 55, 104
Dining rooms, 104
Direct glare, 89, 90, 114
Discharge lamps, 29–39
Display cases, 121
Displays, 88, 119–21
Downlights, 49, 96, 97, 119
Drive-up windows, 123

Efficacy, 7
Efficiency, 7, 39, 41
  fixture, 61, 65, 70
  fluorescent, 30
  incandescent, 15–17
  versus life, 41
Electrical rates, 59
Electrical Testing Laboratories (ETL), 32
Electromagnetic spectrum
  divisions, 2
  light in, 2, 4
Electronic ballasts, 33
Emission mix, 31, 38
Energy-saving methods, 60
Equivalent sphere illumination (ESI), 89

Erythemal energy, 2, 4
Eye, sensitivity, 5

Fading, 119, 121
Failure, filament, 17
  fluorescent, 31
  high-intensity discharge, 38
Far ultraviolet, 2, 4
Filament lamps, 15–29
  advantages, 28, 39
  bases, 17
  depreciation, 17
  disadvantages, 29, 39
  efficiency, 15–17, 41
  energy, 15
  failure, 17
  heat, 15
  infrared, 15
  life, 15
  long-life, 15–17
  low-voltage, 17, 20
  quartz, 27, 28, 39
  rough-service, 25
  three-way, 25
5-by-5 module, 92, 109, 113
Fixtures, 46–53
  bathroom, 99, 102
  calculating, 61–72
  catalogs, 65–69
  chandeliers, 49, 104
  control media, 90
  downlights, 49, 96
  efficiency, 61, 65
  fluorescent, 46, 58, 59
  high-intensity, 50
  high-intensity discharge, 52, 53, 112, 118, 119
  incandescent, 48–50, 58, 59
  indirect, 48, 52, 112, 114
  industrial, 46
  layout, 73–75
  pole, 50
  pull-down, 48
  sconces, 50
  spacing, 73–75
  strip, 46, 50, 118
  structural, 50, 96, 98, 99
  surface-mounted, 48
  track, 49, 96, 97
  troffer, 46, 118
  wall-washing, 80, 82
  wraparounds, 46, 90, 111
Flood lamps, 18–25
Floor cavity ratio, 62
Floor lamps, 7, 100
Floor reflectances, 96, 110
Fluorescent lamps, 29–35
  advantages, 35, 39
  ballast, 32, 92

bases, 30
breaking, 34
cathodes, 29
circline, list, 135
circuits, 33
colors, 29, 40
dimming, 55
disadvantages, 35, 39
efficiency, 30
emission mix, 31
energy-saving, list, 134
failure, 31
features, 39
1500-milliampere, list, 136
fixtures, 46, 118
  costs, 58, 59
higher-light-output, list, 134
high-output, list, 135
length, 34
life, 34
list, 133
operation, 29
radio interference, 33, 92
shapes, 31
slimline, list, 135
temperature effect, 34
U-shaped, list, 135
Foliage, 106
Food preparation, 88, 101
Footcandles
  average, 70–72
  decrease, 70
  definition, 7, 70
  formula, 7, 70–72, 79
  initial, 79
  levels, 5, 75, 76, 86–88
  measurement, 86
  point-by-point, calculating, 79
  range, 5
  recommended, 71, 75, 88, 118
  source, 71
  vertical, 117, 118
Footlambert, 7, 8
Formulas
  candlepower, 81
  footcandle, 7, 70–72, 79
  footlambert, 8
  inverse square law, 79
  lumen, 71
  maintenance factor, 70
  reflectance, 9
  room cavity ratio, 62
Frequency, 2
Furniture reflectance, 110

Germicidal energy, 2, 4
Glare, 89, 90, 108, 114
  direct, 89, 90
  indirect, 89, 90, 112

reduction, 90
source, 89, 90, 115
video screen, 90, 114
Glass, 8
Grooming, 99, 102–4

"Half-the-light" rule, 81
Halogen cycle, 27
Heat lamps, 26
Hertz, 2
High-intensity discharge (HID), 35–38
  failure, 38
  fixtures, 52, 53, 112, 118, 119
  operation, 35
  parts, 35
High-intensity discharge lamps, 35–38
  advantages, 39
  disadvantages, 39
  features, 39
  high-pressure sodium, 35, 37, 39
  mercury, 35, 39
  metal halide, 35, 37, 39, 112, 118
  operation, 35
  3000 degrees Kelvin, 37, 118
High-intensity lamps, 50
High-pressure sodium lamps, 35, 37–39
  color, 38, 39
  failure, 38
  in fixtures, 52, 111
  list, 132
  ultraviolet, 35
Homes, 95–107
  design steps, 95
Hospitals, 124

Incandescent lamps, 15–29
  advantages, 28, 39
  bases, 17
  disadvantages, 29, 39
  efficiency, 15–17, 41
  energy, 15
  failure, 17
  features, 39
  fixtures, 48–50
    costs, 58, 59
  heat, 26
  infrared, 26
  life, 15–17, 41
  list, 126, 136
  low-voltage, 17, 20
  quartz, 27, 28, 39
  rough-service, 25
  three-way, 25, 26
  vibration service, 26
Illuminating Engineering Society, 87
IES Lighting Handbook, 87
  recommended light levels, 76
Indirect fixtures, 48, 52, 94, 112, 114
Indirect glare, 89, 112, 114

Indirect lighting, 94, 112, 114
Industrial fixtures, 46
Infrared, 2, 15, 29, 92
Initial costs, 57
Initial footcandles, 79
Instant-start circuit, 33
International Commission on Illumination
    (CIE), chromaticity diagram, 14
Inverse square law, 20, 79–81
    applications, 80
    cosine table, 80
    example, 79, 82, 83
    formula, 79
    illustrated, 79
    to choose source, 81
Ironing, 104

Kelvin, 11, 12
Kitchens, 88, 101, 102

Lamp, 7, 15–41
    calculating number, 61–85
    catalog, 126–36
    choice, 39, 75
    incandescent, 15–29, 39
    flood, 18–25
    fluorescent, 29–35
    high-intensity discharge, 35–38, 39
    lumen depreciation, 70
    mercury, 35, 39
    metal halide, 35, 37, 39, 118
    mortality curve, 16
    ozone, 4
    portable, 7, 48, 98
    reflector, 18–23
    quartz, 26–28, 39
    selector, 39
    shade, 48, 49, 98
    summary, 39
    table, 7, 48, 103
Layout, fixture, 73–75
Length, fluorescent, 34
Lenses, 90
Libraries, 122
Life, incandescent, 15–17, 41
    efficiency effect, 15
    end, 17, 31, 38
    fluorescent, 34
    long, 15–17
    rated, 16, 41
    tolerances, 16
    versus efficiency, 41
    voltage effect, 17
Light, 2–5
    black, 2, 3
    bulb, 15–41
    control, 42–45, 90
    cost, 57–60
    definition, 4
    division, 2, 10

levels, 5, 75, 76, 86–88
    calculating, 61–85
    low, 89, 95, 108
    table, 88
    meter, 86, 87
    output, 7
    polarization, 42, 90
    quality, 89–91
    quantity, 86–89
    reduction, 70
    reflectors, 8
    source, choice, 39, 75
    wavelengths, 2
    white, 12, 14, 29
Lighting, 61–125
    applications, 92–125
    bathrooms, 88, 99, 102
    controls, 54–56, 60, 90
    costs, 57–60
    design method, 75
    dining rooms, 104
    energy-saving, 60
    foliage, 106
    grooming, 99, 102–4
    homes, 95–107
    indirect, 94, 112, 114
    ironing, 104
    kitchens, 88, 101, 102
    level, recommended, 71, 75, 88, 118
    merchandising, 117–21
    offices, 88, 108–16
    outdoors, 105
    paintings, 100, 101
    plants, 106
    private offices, 115, 116, 123
    quality, 89–91
    quantity, 86–89
    residences, 95, 107
    schools, 88, 121
    sewing, 104
    sinks, 96, 97, 101
    stores, 117–21
    study, 104, 122
    systems, 111
    task/ambient, 112
    trees, 105
Lamp lumen depreciation (LLD), 70
Loading docks, 88
Long-life lamps, 15–17
Louvers, 45, 90, 111, 115
    parabolic wedge, 45, 90, 111, 115
Low-pressure sodium, 35, 38
Low-voltage controls, 54
Low-voltage filaments, 17, 20
Lumen, 7
    calculating, 71, 72
    depreciation, 70
    method, 61–75
    R and PAR lamps, 19
Lumens per watt (LPW), 7, 41

Luminaire dirt depreciation (LDD), 70
Luminaires, 46–53
Luminance, 7
Luminous ceiling, 52, 96, 111

Machine reflectance, 110
Maintenance, 60
Maintenance factor, 70, 71
  formula, 70
  source, 71
Makeup, light for, 102, 104
Merchandising, 117–21
Mercury lamps, 35, 39
  color, 37, 39
  failure, 38
  list, 132
  self-ballasted, 37
  store use, 118
Metal halide lamps, 35, 37, 39, 118
  color, 37, 39
  failure, 38
  group relamping, 113
  in fixtures, 52
  list, 132
Meter, light, 9, 86, 87
Middle ultraviolet, 2, 4
Mirrors, 99, 102, 103
Module, 5-by-5, 92, 109, 113
Moonlight, 5
Mortality curve, 16
MR-16, 28
Multiplier, 49

Nanometers, 2
Near ultraviolet, 2, 3
Nurses stations, 124

Office, 88, 108–16
  5-by-5 module, 92, 109, 113
  glare, 108, 112, 114, 115
  lighting systems, 111, 112
  open plans, 113
  private, 115, 116, 123
  reflectances, 110
  seeing tasks, 108
Operating costs, 58
Outdoor lighting, 105
Outer jacket, 35
Ozone lamps, 4

Paint reflectance, 8
Paintings, 100, 101
Parabolic louvers, 45, 90, 111, 115
Parking garages, 88
PAR lamps, 18–25
Patient rooms, 124
Photocells, 55
Piano lights, 50
Picture lights, 50, 100
Pigment, mixture, 10

Plant light, 29
Plant lighting, 106
Polarization, 42, 44, 45, 90
Pole lights, 50
Portable lamps, 7, 48, 98, 100
Preheat circuits, 33
Private offices, 115, 116, 123
Problem, sample design, 76
Productivity, 87, 88, 108
Pull-down fixtures, 48

Quartz lamps, 26–28, 39, 131

Radio interference, 33, 92
Rapid start, 33
Rates, electrical, 59
Recommended footcandles, 71, 75, 88, 118
Reflectance, 8, 10, 96, 110
  aluminum, 8
  ceilings, 95, 110
  concrete, 8
  enamel, 8
  floors, 96, 110
  formula, 9
  furniture, 110
  glass, 8
  machines, 110
  materials, 8
  measuring, 9
  paint, 8
  stainless steel, 8
  walls, 96, 110
  wood, 8
Reflected glare, 89, 112, 114
Reflection, 42, 43
Reflection factor, 8, 10
Reflector lamps, 18–23
Refraction, 42
Residences, 95–107
Restaurants, 88, 121
RLM fixtures, 46
Room cavity ratio, 62–65
Room surfaces, 96, 110
Rough-service lamps, 25
Row spacing, 73, 78
Rules of thumb, 81–85
  caveats and limitations, 81
  "half the light," 81
  "square feet per . . .," 84
  "watts per square foot," 84
  wiring cost, 57

Schools, 88, 121
Sconces, 50
Seeing, 5, 6
  factors of, 6
  task location, 62, 64
  tasks, 89, 108
Self-ballasted mercury, 37
Sewing, 104

Shade, 48, 49, 98
Shielding angle, 45
Shop lights, 46
Show windows, 120
Sinks, 96, 97, 101
Size; as factor of seeing, 6
Slimline, 33
Sodium lamps
    high-pressure, 37, 38
    low-pressure, 35, 38
Soffits, 51, 52, 99, 102
Solid state ballasts, 33
Sound ratings, 32
SP30, 29
SP35, 29
SP41, 29
Spacing criterion (SC), 65, 68, 74
    fixtures, 68, 74
    to mounting height (S/MH), 65, 74
    rows, 68, 73
Spectral power distribution, 12, 13
Spectrum, 2
    parts, 2
    sources, 41
    visible, 2–5
    wavelengths, 2
Speed, as factor of seeing, 6
Spotlights, 120
"Square feet per . . ." rule, 84
Stainless steel, 8
Stairways, 88
Starter circuit, 33
Stores, 88, 117–21
    lighting systems, 117–20
    light levels, 118
    valances, 118, 119
Stove lights, 100
Strip fixtures, 46, 50, 118
Structural fixtures, 50, 96, 98, 99
Study areas, 104, 122
Sunlamps, 4
Sunlight, 5
Supplementary fixtures, 60
Surface-mounted fixtures, 48
Switching, low-voltage, 54

Table lamps, 7, 48, 103
Task/ambient lighting systems, 112
Teller stations, 123
Temperature
    color, 11, 12, 40
    effect, fluorescent, 34

rating, ballast, 32
Terms, 7–9
3K high-intensity discharge lamps, 37, 118
Three-way lamps, 25, 26
Timers, 55
Track fixtures, 49, 96, 97
Transmission, 10, 42, 43
Trees, 105
Trigger start, 33
Troffers, 46, 111, 118
Tungsten, 17

U-shaped lamps, 31, 113
Ultraviolet, 2–4
    erythemal, 4
    far, 4
    germicidal, 4
    "light," 44
    middle, 2, 4
    near, 2, 3
Underwriters Laboratories (UL), 32

Valances, 50, 51, 96, 98, 99, 119
Vertical footcandles, 117, 118
Vibration service lamps, 26
Video display terminals (VDT). *See*
        Cathode ray tubes
Visible spectrum, 5
Visual comfort probability (VCP), 91
Voltage effect, 17

Wall brackets, 51, 96, 98, 99, 116
Walls, reflectance, 96, 110
Wall sconces, 50
Wall-washing, 80, 82
Warehouses, 88
Warm white, 29
"Watts per square foot" rule, 84
Wavelength, 2
White
    ceilings, 92
    fluorescent, 30
    light, 12, 14
    paint, 8
Windows
    drive-up, 123
    show, 120
Wiring cost, 57
Wood, 8
Work plane, 62, 64
Wraparounds, 46, 90, 111